BREAKING
THE RULES
OF PAIN

BREAKING THE RULES OF PAIN

DISCOVER THE ROOT CAUSE
OF CHRONIC PAIN SO YOU
CAN FLOURISH AND GROW

AMIE RULE

First published in 2024 by Dean Publishing
PO Box 119
Mt. Macedon, Victoria, 3441
Australia
deanpublishing.com

Copyright © Amie Rule

All rights reserved. No part of this publication may be reproduced, stored in a retrieval system or transmitted in any way or by any means, electronic, mechanical, photocopying, recording or otherwise, without the prior written permission of the author and publisher.

Cataloguing-in-Publication Data
National Library of Australia

Title: Breaking The Rules Of Pain — Discover the Root Cause of Chronic Pain So You Can Flourish and Grow
ISBN: 978-1-925452-99-0
Category: Self-help/healing
Self-help/pain management

The views and opinions expressed in this book are those of the author and do not necessarily reflect the official policy or position of any other agency, publisher, organisation, employer or company. Assumptions made in the analysis are not reflective of the position of any entity other than the author(s) — and, these views are always subject to change, revision, and rethinking at any time.

The author, publisher or organisations are not to be held responsible for misuse, reuse, recycled and cited and/or uncited copies of content within this book by others. This book and its remedies or opinions act as a personal guide only and are not to be used without appropriate consultation with your doctor or health care practitioner. This book is not intended as a substitute for the medical advice of physicians. The reader should regularly consult a physician in matters relating to his/her health and particularly with respect to any symptoms that may require diagnosis or medical attention. The ideas within this book are only the opinion of the author and are not intended to replace any medical advice or diagnose health issues. This publication is meant as a source of inspiration and information for the reader, however it is not meant as a substitute for direct professional assistance and is not to be construed as professional advice on medical, legal, technical or therapeutic matters.

No part of this publication may be reproduced, stored in a retrieval system or transmitted in any way or by any means, electronic, mechanical, photocopying, recording or otherwise, without the prior written permission of the author.

For all the women who continue to
courageously break the rules.

For my kids who taught me about unconditional
love and to courageously show up as myself.
Thank you for being my biggest teachers.

Contents

Introduction:
I Know Why You Are Here ~ 1

Part 1:
Understanding Where the Rules Came
From – Redefining Trauma ~ 7

Part 2:
A Tale of Pain, Discovery, and Healing ~ 23

Part 3:
Unravelling Chronic Pain ~ 101

Part 4:
Raised to Believe ~ 173

Part 5:
Integrated Healing ~ 217

Acknowledgements ~ 313
About the Author ~ 317
Endnotes ~ 318

Introduction

I KNOW WHY YOU ARE HERE

Not another self-help book, you might be thinking. Thankfully, this book is so much more. Within these pages lie the life-changing resources to help uncover the meaning and true source of your pain. You'll learn how to listen to its message and, most importantly, how to nurture your body's pain and foster healing.

It has taken me a lifetime of battling chronic pain and 15 years of personal development to unravel all the pieces of this puzzle and put them together in a cohesive framework. An all-inclusive framework that I can share with others so they can arrive at a better place, a better life so much sooner than I did. I was compelled to do all this work myself because there's still so little research and information available around how to treat, manage, and heal from long-term, chronic pain, despite the increase in incidences of people living with chronic pain.

The resources and knowledge I have collated here combine personal experiences with both Eastern (holistic practices) and Western (scientific) medicine principles to help you embrace a new reality. My aim is to create a reality shift to help you see that all the rules you've been told about the pain you experience, the condition you may have, and the diagnosis given to you **aren't true**! You are not incomplete. You are not broken. You do not need fixing.

I can hear you say, "But how is that possible? I have an autoimmune condition. I have an invisible illness. I suffer from inescapable pain. I suffer from debilitating fatigue. The life that I once had is gone. The pain keeps me trapped."

I understand. I too have experienced all of this. For decades, I was focused on the perspective that I was 'without', that I was incomplete without my physical health, that there was something wrong with me, that I too needed to be fixed. This caused me to feel immense shame, and, as a result, I isolated myself from the vast society of seemingly 'normal' people. It caused me to hide my pain from so many while simultaneously chasing practitioners who I prayed could 'fix' me, only to discover that they could neither locate the cause of my pain nor heal it. As my symptoms continued to get worse and my diagnoses increased, I spiralled further down the shame cycle, thinking that I was at fault. The self-blame was prominent, and the mental, emotional, and physical pain engulfed my entire existence. I couldn't remember a time when I was without pain. My pain defined my life. It prevented me from going to work, from socialising, from exercising, and from living and experiencing a normal life.

The continual focus on my pain and suffering caused me more pain and suffering. It was a cycle I couldn't break out of.

For those of us who have had to endure any type of persistent pain, we know how debilitating it can be and how desperate we become to shift the pain and make it go away. Our approach can be quite symptomatic. That is, we look at reducing the symptoms to reduce the pain within our body and mind. Too often, doctors and specialists are quick to prescribe medication for the pain, which, in reality, is only helping to mask it. The pain then lies dormant, just waiting to be triggered again, and it always comes back with a vengeance.

Different specialists told me it was all in my head, that it was psychosomatic, that the symptoms and the pain weren't real. I felt disheartened, defeated, and at a total loss. I lost faith in the system and also in myself and my body. After so many years of searching for an answer to why I was constantly experiencing pain and wishing my experiences could be validated, specialists finally told me they had finally 'found' a diagnosis. At first, they told me to fight it. Then they told me to live with it. Then they told me to take a pill to suppress it, or painkillers to mask it. Yet despite taking painkillers and anti-inflammatories and dabbling in antidepressants, the physical pain continued and intensified.

It didn't matter what I tried; nothing seemed to shift it. I become stuck and stagnant, feeling a sense of shame, embarrassment, and failure. This wasn't how my life was supposed to be. I was stuck in a cycle of 'why me': *Why is my life so hard? Why do bad things keep happening to me?* But I was looking at it from the wrong direction and following the wrong rules.

Out of all the information I was bombarded with, I eventually discovered something inherently missing in the consultations I had faithfully believed in for so long.

Nobody told me I needed to listen to what my body was telling me. Nobody told me I was perfectly formed and did not need fixing.

I could not have known then that I was another casualty of a set mindset that could only see life as happening *to* me, where it seemed I was the victim and had little control over how my life was playing out. At the time, the fight for a diagnosis, the fight for my existence, the fight to be heard, to be validated, and to be seen caused an immense amount of burnout and fatigue. I soon had little fight left in me. I was so tired and felt powerless, defeated by a system that didn't seem to understand me and didn't know how to guide or support me.

For so long, I had been giving my power to those around me in an attempt to receive a diagnosis, to take away my pain and fix me. And when they couldn't, I felt more broken than ever. I felt like a prisoner within my own body. It felt like a life sentence. I didn't know that I had any power to do anything about what was happening in my life.

So, after many years of experiencing numerous dead ends and ineffective treatments from a Western medicine perspective, I was compelled to keep exploring well beyond this conventional yet confined set of rules to find the cause of my pain. By exploring the vast array of other teachings and healing techniques – many of which are much older than Western medicine – I found a treasure trove of possibilities. Finally, I discovered what I needed to know and accept to move past the mindset I had been stuck in for decades.

I discovered I was a by-product of my environment, past and present, and my experiences, past and present.

Therefore, everything about me – my life, my thoughts, my beliefs, my assumptions, my perception of the world, my relationships, and my emotional states – had directly impacted my body, mind, and spirit in multiple capacities. A pivotal turning point for me was understanding that the pressure, stress, and emotion around these factors have an enormous physical impact on the body and its 'normal' functions.

These pressures and issues that we feel physically, day after day, heavily influence how we carry and interpret pain within ourselves, even to the point that what we are doing and thinking creates more pain. Until you find the knowledge – the very knowledge in this book – that helps you break those rules of pain that so many of us blindly operate under, these factors will continue to create the chronic pain you live with and believe is part of you.

That used to be me – but not anymore.

Part 1

UNDERSTANDING WHERE THE RULES CAME FROM – REDEFINING TRAUMA

Once I started questioning where pain originated, the answers kept sending me further and further back into my very beginnings. Delving into my childhood, I realised how stress and trauma early on had created a survival response in me. I learnt that a lot of my childhood was spent experiencing a prolonged fear-based response, and this heightened state impacted my development in so many ways – I don't think I've even found them all. I extensively researched the state of stress in humans and quickly learnt that trauma is not only tied to commonly accepted traumatic events, such as going to war, but the trauma actually stems from our reaction (short- and long-term) to the event. Most alarming was realising that stress and trauma only need to be *perceived* as stressful to the individual. Today, we understand that trauma is a subjective experience defined as anything that causes a big shock to our nervous system, activating the fight-or-flight response.

> Each and every one of us has experienced trauma and stress to some degree.

It could be back when we were infants, crying for comfort and not receiving it when required. It could be injuring ourselves, carrying that memory and subsequently creating a fear response attached to the incident. It could be in relation to how we were parented or how we didn't receive the basic fundamentals required for survival as human beings, such as food, safety, and security or, even more pertinent, how we didn't receive the love, nurture, and encouragement required to grow, develop, and evolve positively as children and teenagers. Trauma could also relate to how we were treated at school and if it was a positive or negative experience. Young teenagers now have to grapple with different forms of bullying thanks to social media, which is creating further stress in a form that's new to us and even more unrelenting. Then, of course, there are also big life tragedies that cause immeasurable amounts of stress.

Despite the stress level varying across all these experiences and differing for each individual, the memory and shock of these events have many repercussions. The memory is often imprinted and etched in our conscious memory and stored deep within our subconscious; the scarring goes deep into our psyche and cells.

If the memory of the trauma is retriggered, or the experience is reoccurring, it can have a prolonged impact on the individual. To protect ourselves emotionally from the experience, we instil coping mechanisms that we believe will protect us, such as numbing, blocking, and alcohol consumption. However, using these in the long term doesn't enable us to deal with the trauma. Instead, we create unhealthy behavioural patterns and responses to keep us safe and functioning. If we aren't given the tools to process and release the trauma, it builds up and manifests as something bigger within our body and mind.

INTERGENERATIONAL TRAUMA

Added to the trauma we experience in our own lives is the baggage we carry from the generations that came before us. Many of us don't realise how significantly it affects how we were raised and how we are raising our own children. There is now growing research and evidence around the extent of the effects of trauma that's passed subliminally from one generation to the next. Despite the original trauma occurring one or more generations prior, similar traits and coping mechanisms can be seen across different generations. The effects of intergenerational trauma compound on families and individuals and are often not recognised, understood, spoken about, or dealt with.

My story and that of my birth mother share a similar theme in the sense that she was an orphan raised in an orphanage. I, too, was repeating the cycle, literally birthed into an orphanage and destined to have a life similar to hers until I was adopted. Although I was given the opportunity to change my story and disrupt the generational cycle, the mental, emotional, and physical anguish was still passed on to and imprinted in me. Despite being raised in a loving home, the majority of my life was riddled with feelings of rejection and not being worthy enough. As a recently remarried parent, I often see some of these patterns repeating in my children. However, by having conscious awareness of what's happening, I have the capacity to stop the cycle from repeating and turn the narrative around for my children.

EPIGENETICS

There are also fascinating emerging studies around epigenetics, which is the study of how our environment influences our behaviour, which in turn can actually alter the expression of genes. Ultimately, this means that the genes inherited from our biological parents can be altered and rearranged depending on the environment and our experiences. This also means that our genetic markers can be impacted by positive experiences, such as loving and supportive relationships, or, conversely, negative influences, such as environmental toxicity or stressful situations. These markers can switch genes off and on.

Research also explores how our childhood experience can impact our development and our view of the world and, if filled with trauma, can have a drastic impact on our development.[1] Children are particularly sensitive to these changes. I believe there's an important link yet to be fully explored between how childhood trauma influences changes in the body and goes on to trigger chronic pain and disease. Researchers are starting to see the link between trauma and the nature of health-related conditions and disease, yet there seems to be a lack of focus on chronic pain.

TOXIC LOAD

Finally, we must acknowledge the stress and trauma modern living causes within the body. I call this the 'toxic load', which refers to the entire collection of factors and experiences that create a burden on the entire body, including our mind and emotional body. Toxic load includes factors that can be environmental, social, biochemical, and even related to societal and parental expectations.

These pressures add to the body's mental, physical, and emotional load, which is not seen with the naked eye, making it very hard to detect. Many of us aren't given the skills in school or society in general to deal with the immense load day by day, and we often don't have the mechanisms required to lessen its weight. We only have to look at the increased rate of mental health issues within our younger kids and adolescents to know that something is affecting them that we can't see. Beneath this mystery is the developmental layer that includes variables such as our genetic make-up, our upbringing, and generational trauma. These all affect our perception of the world and heavily influence our mental and emotional wellbeing and resilience.

So many of us experience stress and trauma at monumental levels, activating a continual stress response in the body. To combat this stress, our body undertakes numerous physiological changes, including in the brain and the nervous system. Still, unfortunately for many of us, the extent of stress is too much for the body to deal with, and over time this results in a build-up of physical symptoms. When the symptoms become prolonged, undefined chronic pain starts to arise.

UNEARTHING ANSWERS IN THE PANDEMIC OF PAIN

My motivation for searching for the answers behind today's pandemic of chronic pain will become clear as I share my story with you. My pain, my limitations, my defence mechanisms, and my limited mindset were all lessons I had to acknowledge and explore on my journey that began in a Hong Kong orphanage and continued when I had to adapt to a new life in Australia when a beautiful Perth family adopted me at the age of 5. Although I was incredibly lucky to receive a fresh start with a loving family in a beautiful country, it didn't mean the end of my challenges. Instead, it was the beginning of a different set of challenges.

> When I was at my lowest physically, mentally, and emotionally, something lit up within me about the correlation between the human mind and the body: our mind and our thoughts have the power to impact our physical body.

Over time, I pieced together how pain within my physical body (brought on by perceived stress) would seemingly remain trapped and then expand to impact my nervous system and even the functioning of my brain, as the pain altered the signals my brain was sending to the rest of my body.

I was compelled to explore the complex web and intricate layers of the human body. Many of us haven't been raised or taught to understand the link between how experiences, thoughts, and emotions can be harboured within our physical body, creating certain symptoms and behavioural patterns.

> If the challenging emotions aren't resolved, they can manifest as pain, health conditions, fatigue, and disease.

We must be attuned to our mind-body connection daily; otherwise, the residual tension can cause further inflammation and pain that becomes harder to diagnose as each new ailment that arises seems unrelated to the original issue. Each diagnosis can contribute further to our mental, physical, and emotional state and decline.

Pain, whether physical, mental, or emotional, arises for a reason and is our body's way of communicating to us. Often, long-term pain triggers a subconscious disconnection (between our mind and our body) as a coping mechanism so we can get through each day.

However, the potential by-product of this disconnection or suppression can be debilitating levels of depression and anxiety. For years, I experienced bouts of physical pain and flare-ups that would bring me to a standstill for weeks on end. I would hate on myself and my body and then hate on the world and all those around me who had a seemingly 'easy' life. I would compare myself to others and fall into a vicious cycle of psychoanalysing myself while I fell prey to self-pity. Even more, I fell prey to wounded archetypes that caused me to remain the victim.

Nowadays, I notice the patterns of self-judgement and self-destruction and can separate myself from them. Over time, I've learnt to focus on self-compassion, allowing myself to be human and feel the full spectrum of feelings and emotions, in whatever form they present themselves. These emotions can include anger, frustration, and resentment. However, instead of allowing my ego to take over and tell me I'm not good enough or that my body has failed me or, even worse, that my life isn't worthwhile, I sit within the emotion and allow it to pass by with some level of compassion and grace.

I acknowledge and thank my body for communicating with me to let me know how she needs to be supported. I listen intuitively to what she requires and implement strategies to help support her. I go inward before I go outward and seek support from my community of practitioners who help to continually support my mind and physical and emotional body.

From my own struggles and lessons, as well as the knowledge I've gained from completing my psychology degree, studying psychotherapy, much personal research, my quantum energy and integrative coaching certifications, and especially through working extensively with my clients as a health and energy coach, I've learnt so much about the flow-on effects of pain. This is what I've learnt:

- Pain can cause us to distrust our body.
- Pain can cause us to disconnect from ourselves, our family, and our community.
- Pain can cause us to disassociate from ourselves.
- Pain can keep us trapped in our lifestyle and within emotional and mental patterns.
- Pain can impact us physically, mentally, emotionally, and energetically.
- Pain can cause us a whirlwind of tangled emotions.
- Pain can be the embodiment of childhood trauma.

- Pain can be a trigger and can also trigger a sense of unfilled emotional needs, for example, self-worth.
- Pain can cause survival patterns to arise within us.
- Pain dysregulates the nervous system.
- Pain can change neural pathways and brain function.

The numerous signs and symptoms of pain have the potential to go on and create more pain. If we fight pain, we ultimately end up fighting ourselves and our body, which, in turn, overtaxes our already depleted nervous system.

It is crucial that we embrace an integrated understanding to reach a new level of nurturing and healing our body. We must break down our preconceived and conditioned knowledge of pain (the rules) to rediscover the intrinsic connection between the mind, body and spirit. For me, this has revealed an integrated approach to listening to and healing my whole body. Western medicine has an important role in supporting us, and, as many people do, I turned to it first for help in the early days when I seemingly faced new conditions every few months.

Nowadays, I leverage Western medicine alongside many other modalities as part of my toolkit to help support my body. As you move through the concepts in this book, you will see how, through my own diagnosis and treatment experiences, my awareness grew around the two-way power of a Western medical diagnosis. Of course, we must explore what it can tell us without blindly attaching to it, because it can also create a prognosis that limits us and binds us to what we're 'told' rather than opening us up to what we can discern ourselves through listening to the body and understanding the personal journey it has been on.

There's a fine line between medicine that suppresses the issue identified in a five-minute consultation and finding a doctor or specialist who respects your views, who will work collaboratively with you, who will be open to new ideas, who will seek the wisdom of other practitioners and experts in the field to help find the cause and source of your pain. This allows for different healing perspectives and means you find someone who aligns with your views and beliefs. Treatment like this is also incredibly affirming on an internal level.

We all need practitioners who empower, instead of disempower, with their diagnoses and approach.

Often, we aren't given or made aware of the tools to process our diagnosis, the loss and grief that may come with it, the adjustment necessary to our lives, the shift in expectations of ourselves and our body, and how to recognise the people who can support our mental health to create strength and resilience in all areas of our life. We need to change the narrative that our lives are dictated by pain. We need to be empowered to use the pain to propel us to take back the lead in our lives.

I frequently come across the narrative that life is hard, healing is hard, and chronic pain is hard. To this I say, of course, of course. But the more we focus on that, the more we attach to it, and the more we bring it forward into our reality. It becomes who we think we are.

> We only see the hard, and the harder we tell ourselves it is, the more it becomes our reality. We see, feel, and attract the hard.

We can create a new reality. We can learn to not attach to the pain, not allow pain to become all-consuming where it defines who we are, where we forget who we are without it, where the pain becomes co-dependent and we become co-dependent upon it.

To move away from this, we must become deeply inquisitive about the pain, understand why she is there, develop a relationship with her, and even befriend her. We need not be at war with ourselves. We must learn how to accept and surrender while being compassionate in our healing. Fighting ourselves for the rest of our lives isn't feasible, nor is it a great space to be in. **Resisting the pain only causes more pain in the long term.**

The one thing that many practitioners won't tell you is that it's up to you. You need to reclaim the driver's seat; you need to reclaim your power; you need no longer be the victim in your story; you must be the hero; you must change the story, and you must do it now. You need to call in people to support you; you need to believe that you can change and that your body will heal, but the hardest thing is, you need to pull yourself out of the pain cycle. It's up to you. No other person can do the work for you.

This is not to burden you; it's to empower you in all aspects of your life. I can't tell you what you should do; only you know what your body requires. Only you know what's right for you and your body at any given time. To break the rules of pain, you need to be aware of how you were raised and the conditioning you've been exposed to. The person you are today, influenced by so many factors from your past, may be expressing limited thinking in your life. I simply want to show you how to uncover what you need to find in order to connect in a way you've never been taught.

We all wish to heal our pain, but remember: healing doesn't always mean being free from pain. We need to dispel this notion because the reality is that we all have a different benchmark based on how we emerged into this life, and every single person's life trajectory is different. Healing also doesn't mean being free from disease. It does, however, mean having the ability to identify what's presenting within our physical, mental, and emotional body and to honour and acknowledge these without judgement or criticism but with self-compassion and grace instead.

WHAT DOES HEALING REALLY MEAN?

HEALING MEANS...

realising we are *whole*, we are complete, regardless of our pain and physical body. We still have so much power to manage the aspects of our pain that may test us in our daily lives.

HEALING MEANS...

forgiving ourselves for not knowing better until now and forgiving others too (where applicable). It means no longer harbouring old emotions and no longer needing to battle yourself or your life. It means taking charge of your life, no longer allowing the limitations that physical pain may present to have a hold on you. Concentrate on what you can do, not what you can't, and your abilities and appreciation will grow.

HEALING MEANS...

no longer comparing yourself to others who seemingly have it all (for this doesn't serve us). It means making yourself a priority and making better choices to support your body to allow it to heal, grow, and strengthen so you can create a life that better supports you. It means implementing firm boundaries to support your nervous system to rebuild itself, relinquishing the guilt from your past and the worry from your future. It means removing all expectations of who you believe you need to be for your own approval and that of others.

HEALING MEANS...

knowing that you will have good and bad moments – and that's okay! It means acknowledging that today you are doing better than you were yesterday, and if you're reading this book, you most definitely are! It's acknowledging that some moments are hard, and that's okay. We can get through the hard; we're warriors, after all.

LET'S TAKE THIS JOURNEY TOGETHER

Today, I know I'm not alone in this experience of chronic pain, and I know this is why you're here. You're sick of the constant pain and suffering, hiding and feeling ashamed that your life isn't how you imagined. You've come to the realisation that following the same path you've been on for so long is no longer serving you, and I'm so glad you're finally here.

Many discoveries are waiting for you ahead. As you take this journey with me, it will slowly redefine your perspective of pain, which will help you to:

- Look for the true cause/s of your pain (often in surprising places).
- Find the purpose of your pain.
- Nurture your pain as a signal and message from your body.
- Become empowered by your pain.
- Apply new knowledge and strategies that can alleviate your pain.
- Return to the healthier function your body is designed for.

My passion today is sharing the simple but life-changing principles that have largely been lost in the fast-paced development of society in the last few centuries. It was through my very specific circumstances, very specific trauma, and resulting health challenges that I arrived at a wonderful knowledge to help heal the mind, body, and spirit. This approach doesn't suppress symptoms but rather listens to the message that guides us to rest and support our body with what it needs to heal and function that way it was designed.

You can either choose to begin this journey at Part 2 (my personal story), which shows how the pieces of my life puzzle were formed and how I put the puzzle together to end up at the wonderful place where I am now. Or you can open up to Part 3 where we begin to unravel the science and biology behind chronic pain. Part 4 explores the psychology and energy of emotion, and Part 5 offers you healing options to connect with every day.

Part 2

A TALE OF PAIN, DISCOVERY, AND HEALING

Like many, I have little recollection of my formative years. However, unlike many, I don't have a single baby photo of myself. I neither possess one, nor do I think there are any in existence. The lack of photos and memories are very representative of how I entered and existed within this world as an infant – presumably without meaning.

You see, I was born on 12 July 1980, and 33 days after arriving into this world, I was institutionalised at an orphanage. My case notes explain that my birth mother, referred to as Madam Ng, was an orphan herself. At two years of age, she was presented to her adopted parents by her natural parents. Then, at the age of 15, her adoptive father died. Her adoptive mother, who had divorced her adoptive father, remarried and was reluctant to resume guardianship of Madam Ng. Therefore, at 17 years of age, my mother, still a minor, was made a ward of the state and was once again admitted into the orphanage. Upon admission, it was discovered she was five months pregnant, and I was born a few months later. After giving me up for adoption, she was placed in a hostel where rumour has it, she ran away. She was located soon after and discovered to be pregnant with my half-sister, who was born on 13 June 1981, only 11 months after me.

When I look back on her circumstances, who can blame her for what she did? It wasn't a great existence, and just the term itself, 'ward of the state', tells you a lot about how orphans were treated. To give you more context of the time period, once you turned 18 in the orphanage, you were considered an adult, which meant you were required to leave and somehow fend for yourself. The only way single unsupported females could survive back then was to prostitute themselves. There was absolutely no system to support them. While my case notes allude to the fact that my birth mother became pregnant from her boyfriend, it also reports that she was found in a gentlemen's bar. As I look back on this today, I hold no shame. For a while I did, but I'll return to that later.

As a child, I couldn't comprehend how a mother could abandon a child. I had no understanding of the circumstances or context around how that could happen. I just felt unloved, rejected, and unwanted.

A CHALLENGING START TO LIFE

Raising babies in this day and age, especially in the Western world, there's a vast array of information readily available to support not only our babies' health and wellbeing but also our own. There's also so much more awareness of how important the mother-baby attachment is and how it can predetermine how the infant constructs its view of the world and therefore their place within it. If a baby has a secure early attachment with its mother, they are likely to imprint with the knowledge that they are safe within this world. This positive assurance then flows on to every aspect of their development.

Being raised in an orphanage meant that I wasn't given the chance to form a strong bond or connection with my mum or even a primary caregiver. It also meant that, because of this, the constructs I developed were skewed and gave me a false impression that the world wasn't a secure place. It also created an ideal (on an unconscious level) that I had entered the world without a meaningful reason to exist.

Therefore, I developed the following constructs:

- My birth mother didn't want me, so she rejected me. At 5 years of age, it's hard to really construct any other belief. Everything is black and white, and to me this was reality.
- All babies are born in red brick buildings, that is, orphanages. That's how everyone enters the world.
- To be affirmed, you need to be a good girl; otherwise you'll be given away, which was what my birth mother experienced on numerous occasions. If you're good,

someone will adopt you. If you're bad, you won't be liked or accepted, or they'll send you back to the orphanage, so you can't risk being bad.
- If you're adopted, someone must love you. If not, you aren't lovable.
- You must listen and obey all rules. Conforming means a greater chance of being liked, approved of, and accepted.
- Your peers are your family. It's survival of the fittest, so, in order to survive, you must rely on your peers and stay together as a pack.

I have very little history or literature to draw upon regarding my upbringing and who I was, apart from my case record, which depicts that I was a cheeky and mischievous little girl. I loved to play with the cooking and kitchen set and also loved playing with dolls. This is very representative of who I am today. I still love to cook; the kitchen is one of my favourite places within the home, and if I could physically have more babies, I most likely would. I adore babies; I'm quite obsessed with them to be honest.

I love the notion that even early on within such a sterile, loveless environment, the soul aspects of me shined through and were captured as a pure part of my identity, despite the circumstances. Apart from those case notes, there was very little information about me provided to my new family when I was finally adopted. The information that was provided to my adoptive parents was more like a marketing pack, showing a collection of 'happy' staged shots, with a somewhat capable-looking young girl who had potential to grow into somebody. However, beneath the verbiage and the staged photos was a very unhappy, scared, and almost soulless little girl. How can any child fathom entering a world where she doesn't believe she is wanted? But, as it turned out, I *was* wanted.

FATE AND FAMILY

On what seemed like the other side of the world, fate arranged that there was an Australian family desperately waiting for the approval to adopt a Chinese child. The Rule family originally consisted of my mum, my dad, my two brothers, and my sister. My mum knew in her heart's heart that she wanted more children, but unfortunately she wasn't able to physically carry any more, so she opted to adopt. Luck was on her side when she got 'two for the price of one' (me and my half-sister). At least that's what she tells us!

The adoption process and the approval consisted of two intense years of communicating back and forth between my parents and numerous government agencies in Perth, Western Australia and Hong Kong. There were handwritten letters that were sent via snail mail and countless steps my mum and dad endured to prove that they were capable of adopting and caring for children. For them, every step was painstakingly slow. The process was long and arduous, and my parents were basically interrogated to discern their worthiness. They had to prove they not only possessed the mental, emotional, and physical acumen and stamina to adopt two kids but also the financial backing to support them. I still have those letters and correspondence that changed my life, a small keepsake to remind me that someone was willing to do everything they could to adopt me.

My mum was extremely passionate and driven, and she tirelessly tackled the long list that was required to facilitate the adoption process. She spoke to government agencies, case care workers, and anyone necessary to advocate for my and my sister's rights and get the final approval. My dad supported her endeavours, backed her in the fight, and was the financial backbone needed to support the adoption of two young Chinese kids. It was a momentous task, but finally, on 8 June 1985, my half-sister and I were adopted. On that day, I went from being Yuen Yee Ng to becoming Amie Yuen Yee Rule.

Prior to being adopted, my mum had considered what to name each of us. She asked God and was guided to name me Amie, which means 'much-loved one' or 'beloved'. She was told that I would need to constantly hear how much I was loved, yet nothing, and I mean nothing, could have ever prepared her for what was to come, nor *how much* I would need to hear that I was loved.

LEAVING MY OLD WORLD BEHIND

I have no recollection of coming to Australia, yet I can only presume that having my half-sister beside me meant a somewhat easier transition. We didn't know each other in the orphanage – we were only introduced shortly before our adoptions – so we were, in effect, strangers. But having someone who looked like me, who was also Chinese and experiencing exactly the same journey as me, was very reassuring. She gave me a sense of familiarity in a suddenly foreign world. Everywhere I looked was foreign – the people, their faces, their clothes – and every moment, living in a new world, was stimulation overload. My half-sister helped me not feel so alone, and soon we developed a close relationship, becoming thick as thieves. Even though we didn't have the words to articulate all of our thoughts and emotions to each other, we understood each other at a deeper level.

To anyone watching us from the outside, it would have seemed like a chaotic situation. We were like two petrified street kittens who had been caged at first in an attempt to tame and rescue us, yet we two little kittens had never experienced the outside world, so we were fearful of being released into it. At the same time, we were compelled to explore it with the hope that we could fit in somehow.

We also looked like stray kittens, totally unkempt. We were raised in a government orphanage, so funding and resources were the bare minimum. From what my mum tells me, there were four levels within the orphanage that were designated to particular age groups. Each level had a sleeping area with row upon row of cots, an area for eating, and an area for indoor play. The area for eating was also where homework and revision were done. Like school, we were allocated our own desk. Each day, we adhered to a very tight schedule, waking at 7 am, kindergarten at 9 am, 12:30 pm lunch, then rest until 3 pm. Upon waking, it was bath, homework, and revision until 5:30 pm, then games and group programs until 9 pm.

There was also a barren outdoor play area that each age group took turns using. To me, it seemed like a prison system, constantly rotating around to each activity until the next group came along. Suffice to say, we were literally raised within those four walls. We received little social interaction beyond our peers, who were referred to as 'family'. Reports suggest that volunteers may have visited the children, yet these interactions were quite limited.

Nutritional food was scarce. My skin and body reflected how we had been treated within the orphanage. I was a skinny little thing, extremely malnourished. My sternum and rib cage protruded from my chest thanks to diagnosed rickets, which is caused by a vitamin D deficiency, most likely due to lack of nutrition and sunlight. I also had chronic eczema all over my body, and my skin would split and bleed. Our hair had been hacked off and was kept short to minimise nit outbreaks within the orphanage.

My sister, on the other hand, looked more well-loved. She was chubbier than me, which wasn't a hard thing to achieve considering how skinny I was. The caretakers at the orphanage were taken by her cuteness and referred to her as 'Ah Bo', which means 'precious'. Yet she still arrived in Australia with boils all over her body. We spoke not a single word of English, and we didn't speak Cantonese properly either. We spoke a slang version, so communication between us and to our external world was extremely limited.

Thanks to the four walls that surrounded me for the first years of my life, I didn't know that a world beyond the orphanage existed. When I contemplate the childhood that so many people would think of as normal, I realise mine was sterile and bare in every way: it lacked love, connection, security, reassurance, joy, fun, curiosity, and wonder. These fundamental aspects of childhood were non-existent. We didn't have the basic human rights of love, care, and safety. During the first few years in our new home, we learnt not only of the physical neglect of my body but also the emotional neglect.

TRANSITIONING TO A NEW WORLD

On the day we were adopted, my mum and dad took us to a hotel for the night, where we had our very first bath with proper running water, soap, and bubbles. It was absolute chaos for my parents, as our excitement ran so deep we splashed water absolutely everywhere! At 5 years of age, this wasn't only my first bath experience but also the first time feeling soft towels, freshly cleaned pressed clothes, and proper beds instead of cots.

The flight home was sensory overload. We had never been out of the orphanage, so we had never been exposed to crowded places or seen a plane, let alone been on one. We had never seen a flushing toilet, an overhead light, or any lights we could turn on and off ourselves. We had never seen people of different colours and races, nor the smells and tastes of different food. The whole flight consisted of us two little girls running up and down the aisle, wanting to go to the toilet to see it flushing, and my parents repeatedly apologising to the flight attendants. Eight hours later, we finally arrived in the beautiful city of Perth, Western Australia – our new home.

From then on, it was a whirlwind of trying to assimilate into a foreign environment. Our ability to communicate was limited due to language barriers. While we were used to interacting with fellow kids and caretakers, we had never been part of a traditional family dynamic before. I doubt we had even seen any Aussies before! We had never operated in an environment separate from the orphanage. Everything babies and toddlers learn gradually as part of a natural upbringing at appropriate stages of development was thrown at me all at once at only 5 years old. Imagine trying to navigate these foreign challenges with extremely limited processing skills, limited communication skills, delayed development, and little to no emotional awareness. My nervous system was fraught.

Even harder for those around us to witness was how devoid of love our lives had been so far. It became apparent by our behaviour that the orphanage was quite regimented in its operation and provided very little love and reassurance. Everything was done with military precision, and, in order to get kids to behave (because well-behaved kids meant a higher chance of being adopted), discipline and correction were ranked higher than basic primary needs, such as love, hugs, affection, and kisses. Never having received hugs and kisses meant we didn't know *how* to receive them, and we experienced and learnt this for the first time at 4–5 years of age. For the first time, we were learning how to receive love, express love and affection, and hug and kiss our mum, dad, and siblings. For me, this came easily, as I was so desperate for any loving human contact, so much so that my mum remembers that during the early days of my arrival, I would sit on her lap, stroke her chest, and place my head on her breast, desperate to feel her heartbeat and heart connection.

During my university days, while studying developmental psychology, I remember learning of a controversial experiment during the 1950s where psychologist Harry Harlow demonstrated the importance of early childhood attachment, affection, and emotional bonds for human development. Harlow wanted to research the previous theory that babies only attach to mothers for food, thirst, and pain relief. To do so, he explored the impact of deprivation by taking monkeys a few hours after birth and placing them with two different 'mothers'. One was made from soft cloth but provided no food, while the other was made from wire but provided nourishment in the form of milk. Harlow discovered that the infant monkeys preferred to spend time with the soft, comforting, cloth 'mother' and only went to the wire 'mother' for food. Consequently, Harlow and other psychologists revealed that not only was softness and affection the main driver for cultivating closeness but also that mothers fulfilled the inherent need in babies and infants for comfort and security.[1]

It's amazing how even at 5 years old, there was an instinctual need to feel a mother's heart. Due to the lack of affection and closeness experienced throughout my childhood, once I sensed their presence, I was desperate to feel them and to be loved. I was desperate to belong to someone or something. Because of this yearning, I became eager to please in an attempt to be loved and affirmed, a pattern that has followed me for numerous decades. Many have wondered if it's our environment or nature that creates our behaviours. From my experience, I believe both elements play a part.

Along with learning how to love, we also had to learn very basic skills. We were so primal, animal-like in fact. We didn't know basic etiquette, such as how to sit at a table without shovelling food in or how to eat without our mouths wide open. In actual fact, one of my mum's funniest memories is the two of us hurling cutlery across the room due to our disdain at the need to use it; eating with our hands just seemed so much easier. At first, we were also unenthused about trying new food, but then we felt so lucky for the opportunity to experience such an amazing array of different foods. I'm certain this was when my love affair with food started, and I would often be found gorging myself, trying to compensate for so many years of feeling hungry. My mum literally had to say, "Stop eating, otherwise you'll explode!"

We also didn't know how to act unless someone instructed us what to do. For example, each morning, as soon as we woke, we would make our beds and stand beside them, waiting for them to be inspected and for us to receive our next instruction. My mum cried when she first saw us do this, not having realised the severity of our regimented, structured upbringing until then and how indoctrinated two young hearts and minds could become. We immediately relied so heavily on her and everything she showed us and explained to us. Nothing could have prepared her for the heartache of what she saw in us and the heartbreak associated with that.

Our world became sensory overload; absorbing and learning from our surroundings was like a movie stuck on fast-forward. We learnt about family, love, hugs, TV shows, how to swim, how to play and have fun, how to celebrate birthdays and blow out candles, the special feeling of receiving gifts, how to devour an ice cream and hold a Hungry Jack's burger. We learnt how to meet new people, speak English, feel and experience happiness, smile, laugh, love, and receive love. It was the first time in our lives that we experienced a childhood. Before you dwell too much on the childhood that I had lost, for me, it was a childhood gained, because you can't lose what you never had.

Although, in retrospect, deep down I did sense that, even at that early age, many components of my childhood were lost in the orphanage. Hardly having our basic needs met and then all of a sudden being transported into this new world, with strange surroundings, new noises, new situations, new faces, new people, new language, new rules, new dynamics, new structures, was overwhelming to say the least. Every day, there was something new to learn. The sudden desperation of trying to assimilate into my new environment and absorb and process everything was simply too much. On top of this, I also had an underlying fear that I would be sent back. No 5-year-old has the coping strategies to deal with such psychological challenges. Mentally, physically, and emotionally, I wasn't coping.

THE ART OF ADAPTING

The struggle I was experiencing began to physically manifest as seizure-like outbursts. Often, they would occur while I was doing an everyday task. Suddenly, I would go into an uncontrollable fit. Witnessing these episodes, my mum was petrified. She was lost and uncertain about what the fits were and why they were happening. I have no recollection of them apart from the time I was placed in a shower fully clothed to help me come out of an episode. As frightening as these episodes were to my mum, she gradually realised that my nervous system couldn't process the sheer amount of external information it was receiving, and the fits were a way for me to cope by disassociating – that is, mentally leaving my body and cutting myself off from the present. She also discovered that the best thing to do when I had one of these episodes was to hold me tightly so I could feel safe and slowly regain awareness back into my body.

We soon learnt that disassociation was a trauma response. From a psychological and childhood development perspective, 0–5 years is crucial in developing as human beings, how we see the world, and how we determine our place within it. Similar to the experiment that Harlow performed using infant monkeys, if babies and infants are raised in an environment that enables them to feel safe and secure within themselves, this will generally flow on and enable them to develop healthy attachments with others as they grow older, enabling them to have a healthy perception of themselves.

If a baby isn't raised in a loving and secure environment, the opposite can occur. Our first constructs as children are based upon our exposure to our first environments and the attachment style of our parents or primary caregiver.

When babies are part of a secure attachment style, when they have their needs met, feel safe within their environment, and feel loved and secure, this allows them to feel safe within their world, thus giving them enough reassurance to explore their external environment. Research confirms that initial bonding with primary caregivers is crucial to an infant's development and can subsequently have a major impact on their emotional and social development.[2] In those unfortunate cases where babies aren't exposed to loving, secure, and healthy attachments, they develop unhealthy and non-secure attachment styles, which go on to impact future behaviours and relationships.

Despite a lack of love, affection, nurturing, encouragement, praise, and all the things we take for granted as the natural ingredients needed to raise kids, in my rather hostile environment, I quickly learnt to adapt to its demands. In order to do so, I disassociated from my external circumstances, a technique many individuals learn to survive in trauma-based environments.

As humans, we have an amazing ability to soldier on with life even amid the trauma we are experiencing. From a young age, I learnt to adapt to my life's circumstances, and I drew on this skill after arriving in Australia. I learnt from an exceptionally early age that I couldn't express myself, my needs, or my emotions. Instead, I learnt to bottle them up and carry on. However, once in Australia, my lack of ability to communicate and express my needs, combined with the overwhelm and new emotions, initiated such a huge and constant fight-or-flight response that my nervous system went into overdrive and created seizure-like fits. As I learnt to trust my mum, the episodes faded, along with the fear that she would leave me. Unfortunately, there were deeper wounds beneath the surface that would later expose themselves.

LOVE AND TRUST ARE KEY

As I reflect on my childhood in Perth, I see that it was flooded with so much love and so many happy memories, filled with glorious summers and countless days swimming in our pool or at our beach house. I wasn't oblivious to my good fortune, and I never took my new life for granted because the memory of my hard beginnings was never far away.

Even today, I vividly remember the conflict and turmoil I housed within as I grew up. I struggled immensely with my place within the world and where I belonged. After all, if my birth mother didn't want me and I no longer belonged at the orphanage, how could I fit in and belong within a family of white people when I was Chinese? Almost immediately, I struggled with the notion that my mum in particular could not only want me but also love me. I had presumed that if my birth mother had left me, then so could she and my new family. This subconscious fear ran deep within me for most of my childhood.

Identity was also a huge factor. In addition to who I was, I pondered, "Will I ever be and feel normal? Will I ever fit in? Will I ever not be the orphaned or adopted child?"

I often reflect on how multicultural our world is now, but growing up in Perth in the 80s was far different. I felt the imprint of being different and knew I didn't belong, something I've grappled with my entire life. It also didn't help that when I left the orphanage, the caretakers had told me that I was responsible for looking after my half-sister and that we both had to behave; otherwise, we would be sent back. I lived with this incessant fear that I needed to be good, and if I weren't, I would be discarded. As a child, having this constant threat looming wasn't healthy, and it drastically affected how I lived my life.

The fear of being sent back ran so deep that I became the good girl, vowing to always be good. I took on the new role in every way and performed, excelled, and thrived. I thrived on learning new skills, being affirmed and congratulated for each skill gained, being doted upon, being adored by strangers, and receiving the love I had missed out on so far in my life. I soaked it all in, thinking how amazing it was to feel loved. I soon developed the idea that praise meant that I was loved and affirmed, and when I wasn't praised, it meant I wasn't loved or lovable. Praise and words of affirmation were my drug to increase my self-confidence and feel worthy.

Despite the love, praise, and affirmation, deep down inside, I doubted the truth of it. The idea of being loved bounced right off the surface, and the massive hole in my heart remained a gaping void that my family's love couldn't seem to fill. Time and again, I kept trying my hardest to fill that abyss. My mum described me as a hungry little caterpillar trying to eat and fill that void with anything I could find, but, unlike the caterpillar that soon grew its wings, I still felt empty.

Over the years, I tried to fill the emptiness with things like food, displays of love, trying to fit into popular groups, being the good girl and being rewarded and validated for it. Even when I look back to my early adult years, I see that so much of my behaviour was underpinned by my need to be loved, affirmed, accepted, and to feel like I belonged.

Over time, I learnt not just to love my mum but also to trust her. I was so desperate as a little girl to feel a mother's love, yet never having had the opportunity to develop any maternal bonds, it took me years to form the mother-daughter connection that I longed for and to feel the security of trust.

IT'S ALL ABOUT SURVIVAL

Even once my relationship developed with my beautiful mum, my ever-present fear of being sent back led me to start lying to protect myself. I would tell little white lies (like many children do) to avoid getting into trouble, although this in itself got me into trouble anyway. Over time, the lying increased, and I ended up creating different personas to please people.

From a very young age, I struggled with who I was in this world, my existence, why I was born, and my purpose. Being raised in an orphanage meant I didn't experience the usual developmental milestones associated with identity formation. I didn't learn about trust and developing a sense of positive autonomy as a person who still needs the support of loved ones or family. I didn't experience or understand any of this. Instead, I experienced a number of different caretakers whose job was to enforce instruction on me. I rarely received any personal care, let alone the love and attention I craved, so I learnt to rely solely on myself. In such an environment, it was survival of the fittest, and that meant trusting only myself.

After my adoption, I also struggled immensely with the way I looked, knowing that I didn't look like everybody else in a very white society. My body looked different; my facial features (almond eyes, rounded face, flattened nose, yellowish skin) looked different. During adolescence, the impact of malnourishment was constantly present, with my slight frame and chest. Comments would sting and leave an imprint on my self-esteem. Self-esteem issues were never far, and, from as early as I can recall, I despised the look of my body and legs. This carried through to adult life.

As a 6-year-old, I remember when I had to wear a leotard and was disgusted by the image of the person looking back at me in the mirror. From such a young age, I carried so much shame for who I was and how I looked. I looked at my peers longingly and lovingly, wishing I had long, skinny legs like them instead of the short, stumpy Asian ones I had, wishing I had blonde hair instead of dark Asian hair. I longingly wished to be anyone but me.

At times, growing up, I still felt very alone, although having my half-sister beside me gave me a lot of comfort and support. She soon became my ally; after all, we were sisters. She also looked like me, which gave me some certainty in a world where I was surrounded by only Caucasian faces. I couldn't articulate how we were different; I just knew that my sister and I were different from the people around us, and I often represented this in my drawings. I would draw us with round faces and the rest of our family with square faces.

Along with investing years and years trying to reassure me of my place and her love for me, my mum also loved and parented the rest of our family. During my childhood, my parents adopted two more Chinese kids into our family. A few years after my sister and I came a gorgeous Chinese boy (a year older than me) who we absolutely fell in love with and doted on. The three of us became our own little pack and did everything together as kids. Last but not least, a few years thereafter, we welcomed a teenage girl into the family. Every time she adopted another, Mum would sit us down and tell us that her love for each of us would never change and she loved us just as much as ever… and she did, without a doubt.

As adults, we often joked about the Asians taking over the family. For us adoptees, it gave us a good life. In addition, being culturally represented and having a balance of cultures within the family dynamic made us more comfortable in our environment.

As a parent myself now, I wonder how my mum ever managed

to invest so much time in caring for all of us so individually, yet somehow she did. She acknowledges that at times, she didn't cope, as many parents will attest to. Yet she dedicated her life to raising seven children and giving four of us a life we never would have had without her.

At the time, I didn't realise, nor appreciate, the mental, emotional, and physical investment that comes with parenting. Add to that all the additional factors of interracial adoption, developmental considerations, and individual requirements of each child. I also realise how my older siblings (especially my oldest sister) must have taken on roles and responsibilities beyond their ages, caring for all the adopted kids who kept joining our family. I was unaware of the new demands and pressure it placed on each family member and how they were forced to take on roles and responsibilities that were generally beyond their scope. Taking on and accepting a new family member who isn't blood related is commendable. Doing this four times must have been challenging and disruptive to the existing family dynamic.

Despite all of this and despite my internal angst, I had a very happy childhood filled with much laughter and fun. There were many days spent with extended family, my beloved nan, and wonderful friends, days filled with togetherness, celebration, laughter, time spent at our beach house, on our family boat, beside our pool. I cherished my childhood and the time we had in Perth.

I never had a yearning to find my birth mother. As I reflect back, I'm not sure if I was vehemently rejecting this aspect of my life, unwilling to face it, or if I was just so content with where I had arrived that I didn't need to look back. I also know that because my half-sister was beside me, I didn't have that sense of yearning and searching that many adoptees have. Her presence gave me a sense of sharing a part of my origin with her. As I've matured and since becoming a mother myself, I think of my birth mother often. My heart often heaves with heaviness knowing what she had to endure, the sacrifices she had to make in giving up two children, and how heartbreakingly hard it would have been to live her life. Over the years, I've learnt to forgive her and hold her in a place of empathy, as opposed to deep disdain and anger, because I know deep down just how fortunate I am for the life and love I've experienced.

THE REBEL AWAKENS

At 12 years of age, our entire family uprooted to Melbourne. My dad, a very successful property developer, had more business in Melbourne than in Perth, so Mum decided to relocate us, all seven kids, to be with him. The transition was difficult for us all. Melbourne and Perth are polar opposites, from sun-filled, happy beach days to Melbourne's dreary, cold, polluted existence. It was a challenging few years for all of us, as it took us a while to find our place in this foreign city.

Over the next few years, I grew more self-assured. I found my place within my family and within the world. But deep down, I still had an incessant fear of abandonment and unworthiness. I loved my mum; I loved my family. I knew I wouldn't have had a life without them, and I felt gratitude and appreciation, but I also felt a sense of resentment. As the years progressed and my adolescence approached, I, like every teenager, challenged my mum and her authority.

I don't know if my rebellious streak was aligned with the typical development phases of a teenage girl trying to find her place in the world as an individual, if I was protesting against having been the good girl for too long, or if it was an accumulation of all the repressed emotions and anger I had felt for my life to date, or if it was all of the above. Regardless, I decided I would test my mum, and boy did she cop it. I pushed her to her limits to see whether or not she would forsake me, just like my birth mum did.

From a human development perspective, adolescence is a crucial time for developing one's self-identity. In doing so, adolescents generally seek greater independence and autonomy from parents and focus more on social connection with peers.[3] As a child, I wasn't afforded the right environment to enable me to go through the proper development phases in early childhood that would allow me to individuate and achieve my own identity. Because of this, as a teenager, I struggled again to understand who I was and my true identity, which once again triggered me to question where I belonged.

The ingrained structure from the orphanage had taught me that my peers were the closest thing I had to family. I also developed this belief that, just like my birth mum, my mum couldn't be trusted because she too would forsake me. In an attempt to seek greater independence, as I grew older, I rebelled not just against her but my entire family due to the deep-rooted thinking that it was more important to fit in and belong to a social group. This can be a natural compulsion for many teenagers. However, my motivation ran deeper than most. Combine that with the usual teenage angst, puberty, and hormones, and I started to really challenge the status quo at only 12 and 13 years old.

I no longer wanted to be the good girl because, in my mind, I had been the good girl for so long. It was exhausting, and, most of all, it hadn't taken away the vast crushing void in me. Teenagers can be like forces of nature when they're scared, and I fought against the status quo as hard as possible. I started to skip school. I started to hang out with the rebellious crowd. I swore; I smoked; I shoplifted; I hung out with the opposite sex; I became daring. I lost all regard for authority. My grades declined, and I started to have less and less respect for authoritative figures like teachers and my parents.

I was soon suspended and then ultimately expelled. As in any healthy parent-adolescent relationship, there were consequences for my behaviour, which made me rebel even more. I started running away from home, and I would sleep over at friends' houses, lying to their parents about why I was there.

At 14 years of age, I still didn't understand or really comprehend the consequences of my actions, so I continued to challenge the system. Once when I was caught skipping school, I decided not to go home, as I didn't want to deal with the confrontation. Instead, I stayed at a friend's place for three days until my brother tracked me down and took me home. I was so angry at being forced to go home that, after a couple of days, I left again, only to be tracked down again by a family member and made to return. In one instance, my mum called the police and asked them to come and speak to me about the consequences of being a delinquent and living on the streets. A policeman sat in front of me at home, highlighting the reality of living on the streets, urging me to take note and change my behaviour, change my ways.

None of it even registered in my head. It was all just babble, and I believed that nothing would happen to me – the invincibility of a teenage mindset. I was ignorant to all the possibilities of what could happen on the streets. The turmoil and stress took a significant toll on my mum and my family. Mum was physically, mentally, and emotionally exhausted by my continual rejection and hatred towards her and the family. I will also take the opportunity to remind you that I was one of seven children my mum was parenting! She was, is, and always will be a stellar superstar mother.

Underlying it all, I was still trying to fill that big empty hole inside of me, the one I had previously tried to fill with food and love, but now I wanted more, not just to be loved and accepted but to be heard, acknowledged, and affirmed. As the years went by, the emptiness continued to grow. I wanted to belong to a group and be fully accepted for exactly who I was. The lack of self-worth and abundance of self-hatred underlying this were huge, and I hoped that the love from my peers would build me back up.

I didn't know that this had to come from within, so I continued seeking external validation. It took years to understand that the motivation for my behaviour and my disdain for my mum and anyone in authority was the innate fear that my mum would reject me. Although this fear was unconscious, it predisposed me to reject anything and anyone before they could reject me.

My beautiful mum was at her wits' end. As a parent to two young children, I can't even imagine the frustration and pain associated with my behaviour, yet, for so long, she persevered. She did only what she knew how to do, and after praying one day, she felt that she needed to let me leave my family in the correct manner. If this teenage delinquent was so adamant not to be there, she felt it best that I should pack my bags and say farewell to my family. Anyone looking in from the outside would question the logic behind this move, but Mum had to trust her intuition and know that this would be the turning point in my life. She needed to allow me to face the reality of my decisions.

I was livid. I had so much anger bubbling up inside of me. *Who was she to tell me that I could finally leave? Who was she to kick me out of my house?* But I still packed everything I needed, and I left. I had no idea where I would reside or how I would survive, but my stubbornness meant that I wanted to prove to myself and my family that I didn't need them. I truly believed that my friends would support me and they were all I needed. *After all*, I thought, *your peers are your family*.

Not for a moment did I realise just how ignorant I was and what the actual world looked like. The stark reality of my decision hit me. All my so-called friends were at school during the day, and at night they were at home with their parents, a roof over their heads, enjoying a home-cooked meal while I was trying to figure out where I was going to stay. Some of my friends' parents reluctantly agreed to take me in. They had questions and concerns, mainly – who was this girl, rebelling and trying to influence their kids?

Over three days, I went from place to place, realising that this peer-oriented life I had created in my head wasn't real. My friends weren't capable of taking care of me, nor was I. I had never felt so alone and scared, and I was desperate. It felt like all my girlfriends had forsaken me, and I was lost. Desperate times call for desperate measures, and, on the last night of my time away from home, I stayed at a male friend's house. I had befriended him and his brother at church a few years beforehand. They let me stay at their family home that night as the reality of my decision to leave home hit hard.

I was 15 years old, desperately trying to prove myself to the world, but instead I had challenged my mum so much that I pushed her away. I was in the midst of enormous turmoil, trying to contemplate what I had done, how I was going to return home, and what the consequences would be.

As my friends went off to school the next day, they said I could have a shower and then let myself out. I still didn't know where I was going to reside that evening. I felt so much guilt, and I distinctly remember feeling so alone, wishing that someone could have stayed with me and comforted me. I assumed I was alone in the house but soon discovered their father was home. He walked into the bathroom while I was showering and sexually assaulted me. I was raped. I remember literally freezing up, not knowing what was going to happen to me – if he was going to hurt me, if I was going to escape unscathed, or how I was going to ask for help. I remember my awareness completely leaving my body as a coping mechanism. My world came crashing down once again. I, too, was now a runaway delinquent, just like my birth mother. I was repeating the same generational trauma and story and shame as my birth mum.

I have no recollection of leaving the house or how I managed to compose myself enough to get on the train back home. I have no recollection of returning home or the words I spoke to Mum. She told me I was in a very fragile state and wouldn't leave her side for weeks on end.

Everything post that day was a blur. I was on autopilot, survival mode, returning home and asking for forgiveness, trying to get back to normal at home, all while carrying the immense shame of hurting those around me and the fact that if I wasn't away from home, I might not have been in this situation. The overwhelming weight of being sexually abused and not being able to talk about it engulfed me. No matter how much I tried to ignore it and pretend that everything was normal, the guilt of it all ate into me.

This event catapulted me so far from everything I had once believed, from my perception of what was safe within the world and what wasn't. I had assumed that I would always be safe. I was raised to believe that God always looks upon us and protects us. I believed that my family would always be there to protect me, but I soon realised that I had put myself in a vulnerable position where I was no longer safe, even though, regardless of anyone's situation, we should never ever become the by-product of sexual abuse and assault. My sense of security was shattered, and once again I reverted to being that fragile, scared little girl from the orphanage, unaware of whom she could rely on and trust. I quickly learnt that my previous propensity for dissociation was a much-needed crutch to fall back on that enabled me to suppress the pain and the hurt within my body.

For years, I didn't tell a soul about the abuse, keeping it a secret. I hid in my shame, trying to process how acts like this can occur to young girls. *Was it my fault?* I assumed it must have been because if I hadn't been in the wrong place at the wrong time, it wouldn't have happened. I had been raised to believe this, and society had reinforced this notion. I held on to that story for years, believing that I was somewhat responsible for the abuse. As an adult, I cannot fathom how a 15-year-old could ever think she was responsible for the abuse of an adult man, yet this is what society indoctrinates into us. In addition to trying to process the event and trauma, they too are grappling with self-responsibility and how the external world will react, instead of having strong support systems to assist them with the pain of being sexually abused and assaulted. Unfortunately, how people react is such a significant reason why women don't speak up and ask for help.

My life soon became consumed with what I could have done better. Particular questions haunted me. *Did it happen because of my ignorance? Was there a lock on the door? Oh my God, was there a lock on the door?! Could I have prevented this from happening? Why didn't I fight? Why did I allow someone to do this to me?*

The shame surrounding this situation riddled me to the point that I couldn't leave the house for fear of another male even glancing at me. I carried this guilt and shame for many years. It infiltrated every part of my being, every cell, and affected every aspect of my life, including how I perceived men and relationships and, in turn, how I projected this perspective onto others and myself. Ultimately, the little girl within me didn't just feel unloved; she now felt broken. I started to shut off from the world in order to protect myself. In some ways, I just got on with life, but, in other ways, I became reckless. Self-hatred would also rear itself, not only telling me I was worthless but also to blame.

One of the most inspiring aspects of the human condition is how adaptable we can be, especially during conflict. Literature suggests that most trauma survivors are "highly resilient and develop appropriate coping strategies … to deal with the aftermath and effects of trauma."[4] While coping mechanisms are used to simply get on with life, the impact of trauma can have a profound emotional, physical, and even cognitive impact on the human body.

For some, trauma can cause the nervous system to become stuck in the 'on position' – that is, stuck in a continual fight-or-flight mode or a deep-seated 'ready-to-react' mode. Most often, we aren't consciously aware of being in this state, but as the body stays in this constant state of uncertainty, it becomes hypervigilant for long periods, causing immense pressure on the body. For many years, I pushed and strived and suppressed the anger, the pain, and the heartache. My nervous system worked overtime to stop me from crashing and burning from the emotional load of the work it took to keep me surviving day to day.

Unfortunately, subconsciously, a very different story was bubbling beneath the surface, the trauma simmering away. The emotional turmoil of this incident had such a detrimental impact on my body that it caused countless health issues. Over the years, my body literally felt like it was breaking beneath me, yet, unbeknownst to me, she was simply asking for love and acceptance, to be acknowledged, to be heard, to be held and comforted.

MY MANIFESTATION OF PAIN

As time passed, I developed coping mechanisms and the resilience to keep living with the pain. This meant disconnecting from the incident and the emotions associated with it. Over time, I tried confiding in people who I thought were a safe haven to share something so painful and personal. It took all my energy to muster up the courage to be vulnerable enough to share it, but people became so uncomfortable at just the mention of the term 'sexual abuse' or 'rape' that it caused a big emotional reaction in them, causing me to have to minimise me experience or to console them over the reaction I had caused, causing me to feel even more guilt and shame.

In retrospect, I didn't have the maturity to place a trigger warning on such conversations or realise talking about such a topic could elicit such unresolved emotions within people who were often triggered because of their own experiences. This was also the era where women were questioned about their part in such encounters, where women were often vilified based on their appearance and their supposed level of promiscuity. This caused many people who had been sexually abused to never come forward with their stories.

So, I learnt to keep my pain and experiences close to my heart and not burden others with my so-called 'issues'. In trying to manage the pain, I thought I could disconnect from it for it to never reappear. However, I just couldn't hide from it. There were too many news stories involving sexual abuse or rape. Every TV show about a girl who was sexually abused would trigger me. Every time I heard about an elite athlete who was involved in some sort of sexual abuse allegation, I was triggered. Within me, there was a buried voice that wanted to scream at those who dismissed it or implied that it was our fault and somehow we 'had it coming to us', but instead I suppressed my anger even more.

Note: This was the late 1990s, long before the equality, equal rights, and 'me too' movements. It was a patriarchal era, where women were often dominated and these issues were suppressed.

I was a master of dissociating as a trauma response and blocked the aspect of myself that let in the waves of emotions connected to my trauma. She was exiled from my awareness and consciousness. I found that if I could stop myself from thinking about the experience, I was okay. If I felt that the buried me was threatening to emerge, I found ways to push her back down, often through partying, smoking, and drinking.

I vividly remember punishing myself by being reckless. I thought that if others could so easily hurt me physically and emotionally, my life obviously meant very little to them, so, in turn, it represented very little to me. This numbed her and kept her small and silent. If she crept up, the pain she encompassed was too immense for me to deal with. Looking back, I was quite manic and kept myself busy because when we're busy, we're too busy to let the negative thoughts infiltrate, and we can keep up the facade that everything is fine.

As the years went by, I learnt how to live a very happy and normal existence. I worked hard. I enjoyed life. My early 20s were filled with a lot of fun and new experiences with my friends and meeting my soon-to-be husband. We had a great life, marrying in 2008 and saving together to create the foundations we can be proud of today.

Shortly after we married, my health deteriorated rapidly. Up to then, I had only experienced a few episodes of burnout, where I became bedridden for days on end despite feeling I had done nothing to overexert myself. Mind you, I was most definitely burning the candle at both ends, but I was young and dynamic and shouldn't have been crashing and burning so significantly.

Keeping busy was a way to avoid confronting the huge void within me, and instead I excelled at maintaining the facade of living the picture-perfect life. Add the whirlwind of a wedding, buying our first home, and starting a new job – I was getting everything a 28-year-old should desire, yet here I was feeling increasingly exhausted each day.

In 2008, I was diagnosed with glandular fever and experienced the onset of chronic fatigue syndrome. From that point on, I rode a rollercoaster of ups and downs, battling against the incessant fatigue in my body and trying to understand it while attempting to hold on to a normal existence.

However, with my Type A personality (and tendency to people please as a means to receive love and acceptance), I didn't want to disappoint anyone relying on me. Instead of listening to my body and understanding that this condition was asking me to prioritise my health over my work and lifestyle, I decided to instead push through in a blur to ensure that I didn't disappoint and wouldn't be judged, criticised, or discriminated against. Unfortunately, there has always been a stigma associated with such health conditions, especially among females. I didn't want to be defined by my health, so I hid my reality from many people.

To maintain this facade, my then-husband would drive me to work so I could sleep in the car on the way. I would work close to a full day, then sleep in the car again on the way home, all just to make it home in time to eat a quick dinner before falling into an exhausted sleep. The fatigue during this period was immense and constantly seemed to be getting worse. My immune system was struggling; I was having trouble with the onset of severe allergies and had trouble digesting and absorbing food and nutrients.

During this period, I was also diagnosed with neutropoenia, an immune system condition that presents as a low white blood cell count. White cells are responsible for fighting off bacterial infections, so there was a concern that if I acquired an infection, I wouldn't be able to fight it off. There were also talks and concerns around cancer, the need for a bone marrow test alongside multiple blood tests. I was prodded and poked in an attempt for doctors to understand what was presenting in my body and why it was under immense stress, yet there was never anything conclusive. I saw a myriad of specialists, doctors, naturopaths, and alternative practitioners to try to get an idea of what was going on. I was desperate for it not to turn into full-blown chronic fatigue syndrome.

Even in late 2008, there was still so little awareness around integrated health and trauma, and how it can impact the mental, physical, and emotional body to produce conditions such as glandular fever, chronic fatigue, and autoimmunity. I had no idea that suppressing my emotions and my past for so long could be such a contributing factor until much later.

My immune system became extremely compromised, and my body just wasn't coping. I lost a considerable chunk of my life thanks to the fatigue and exhaustion of trying to rebuild my body and my immune system. It impacted every aspect of my life, especially my new marriage. This wasn't what my now ex-husband signed up for. I felt new guilt from living a perfectly fine existence one minute and then having someone need to care for me at such a young age, with such extreme fatigue and immune issues. It was guilt upon guilt, shame upon shame, all manifesting as physical pain.

THE SEARCH FOR HEALING

During this period, I was forced to look at different types of therapies to help rebuild my immunity and physical body. Traditional medicine wasn't providing me with the diagnosis, nor the cause of, nor the explanation for what was occurring within my body. There was also no practical knowledge of how to assist me. They would say things like, "We don't understand what's happening within your body, why your neutrophils are so low. It may be cancer, it may not. You have every allergy possible – we don't know why this is the case all of a sudden."

Little awareness did they or I have around how emotional pain can manifest as physical pain and how emotions (defined as energy in motion), when trapped and stagnant within the body, can cause disease.

Or, more simply, it can be an indication that a body is not *at ease*. Similarly, there was little awareness of how our environment, lifestyle, daily activities, and stresses can impact our health and the myriad of related factors that play into this.

I had zero understanding of how my experiences and the mental constructs I had developed during my formative years were now wreaking havoc in my physical body. I was in a continual state of fight-or-flight, which pounded on my nervous system relentlessly. The anxiety around my long-perceived lack of safety and security, combined with substantial nutritional deficiencies, gut issues, structural issues, and osteopenia, meant my body was forced to pay its dues – a body that was literally breaking beneath me. Along with experiencing fatigue issues, my pent-up trauma was now physically manifesting as chronic back pain.

It is both intriguing and mysterious how each individual manifests their trauma and emotions in their own unique way. For me, this appeared as lower back pain in my early 20s. Up to that point, I had been a generally fit and healthy young adult. Despite a short period of relatively unhealthy behaviour (think late teens and early adult years spent smoking and drinking on the weekends), I did pride myself on being healthy. I didn't take recreational drugs; I exercised; I had a personal trainer; I ate nourishing foods to support my body, and I ensured that I had enough sleep because I was conscious of burning the candle at both ends with work obligations and such, so when my back decided to give way for no apparent reason, I was shocked. After a few weeks of rest and recovery, plus massive doses of painkillers, anti-inflammatories, and antispasmodics to treat the pain and inflammation, I started the process of rehabilitation and strengthening my back.

Fast-forward to my late 20s and early 30s, and this pain cycle repeated a number of times. Despite having regular treatment and trying to build my muscles to support my back, at times it would decide that the stress was all too much and would give way, leaving me unable to walk or function for weeks or even months on end. This often happened during interstate trips or even overseas trips, and by the time I returned home, the pain was so excruciating it would leave me unable to walk properly. I relied on doctors to prescribe pills to manage the pain, and physiotherapists and chiropractors to explain the muscular and structural elements that were failing me.

For years, I travelled from specialist to specialist, desperate for an answer to the pain or a diagnosis to understand, only to receive vague, inconclusive answers. I jumped from sports doctors, surgeons, and pain specialists only to be prodded and poked and then medicated or injected with cortisone. There was no answer behind the back pain.

For many years, I struggled with this physical pain that hounded me. It consumed me; it infiltrated every single cell, and it was relentless. Due to an already weakened immune system, any painkillers I took caused immense gut and stomach pain and horrible disorientation. I would wake up feeling defeated every morning, feeling the fresh pain. I was exhausted from not only living with the physical pain but also fighting the mental and emotional battle.

I felt trapped within a body that I thought hated me; after all, why did she keep breaking down beneath me? I felt immense feelings of disheartenment, disappointment, and defeat, which kept me trapped in a pretty big state of depression, yet outwardly I presented otherwise and masked. I continued to show up and pretend that everything was okay because, after all, life goes on, and I realised that no one enjoys listening to someone always talking about their pain. I felt so alone in my experiences and was desperate for someone who could and would understand my pain and my experiences.

I searched for counsellors and pain clinics, hoping that I could find a support crew, someone to validate my experiences, but I soon discovered that there wasn't anything available. Even today, having practitioners who can validate your experiences is difficult, let alone finding a community to support you. Since then, in the work I do today with clients who live with pain, they tell me that all they want sometimes is for someone to understand them, to allow them to express what they're experiencing, to not necessarily project sympathy but rather true empathy and compassion without judgement or even necessarily trying to fix them. I've also found that true empathy and compassion are often hard to find. Another crucial element is having people around you who can share a similar experience that empowers you and doesn't foster staying trapped within the victim mentality.

All I needed was to be heard, and not finding someone who could truly empathise was a huge slap in the face. I felt alone. I felt unheard, and I was struggling to live with the notion of being trapped in a whirlwind of physical pain that didn't have a diagnosis to explain or even validate it.

One of the most challenging aspects of having fatigue and chronic pain is that, despite your pain, the world happily continues on around you. To me, it seemed like everyone else was seamlessly living their lives. Pain seems to highlight the disparity between those living with it and being restricted or impacted by it, and those who live freely without it (or so we think). The external world was a constant reminder of what I was missing out on. The fact that I was married to a triathlete also didn't help, as watching his physicality and endurance reminded me of my lack of capabilities.

Another challenging part of living with chronic pain and having an invisible illness is society's inability to see you for who you are without judgement. Doctors and specialists would often project judgement because, on the surface, I looked okay. Others would imply that it was all in my head or that I was a hypochondriac. I spent day after day, week after week, trying to find a specialist and medical team that would see and hear me for who I was and not judge me for my symptoms or lack thereof.

I would often leave doctors' appointments feeling defeated and unheard, and most weeks I would fluctuate between hoping not to be judged and discriminated against and desperately wanting to be seen and heard and have someone take the pain away. For too long, I didn't realise this was just a cycle of repeating behaviour. It was no different from the little girl in the orphanage who was desperate to be seen and heard or the teenage girl who had been sexually abused. Fast-forward to my adult self, and there I was in a whirlwind of physical pain and an immense amount of emotional pain, desperately wanting to be seen and heard.

Despite wanting to open up and be heard, my experiences taught me that I couldn't trust and confide in others, which made me isolate myself and close myself off from others and the world and also distrust myself and my body. I remember feeling so alone for so many periods of my life. In the orphanage, I learnt how to self-soothe, and as an adult, I found I was required to do the same, so I did. I got on with life, once again discounting and disconnecting from the aspects of myself that caused me pain.

I learnt to adjust my life around the pain. I stopped asking for help and would only seek it when I was literally incapacitated and unable to walk or function. I worked from home as much as possible so I could rest and nap throughout the day. I altered my job to enable me to stop meeting clients face-to-face, as I had to conserve as much energy as possible and being in client-facing roles meant I couldn't mask what I was experiencing. I stopped travelling so it wouldn't impact my body. I requested a stand-up desk to support my back when I was in the office. I altered my life and stopped going out and socialising after work.

I also stopped socialising with my friends because that too would cause an immense amount of fatigue. The fatigue was so significant that I could barely maintain enough energy to get through the working day. I lost joy. I lost any creativity I had. For years, I survived within my pain, which seemed too much to bear, let alone share. I was afraid that if I ever let it out, it would be all too much for not only me but also for the person I shared it with. I knew that people usually pity those who have endured trauma and pain, and I didn't need pity; I needed love. I just kept pushing through.

FINDING JOY AMID THE PAIN

Not only did I adjust my life, but I also adjusted my expectations of how my life should be. My focus intensified on pushing through the pain, suppressing it, ignoring it, fighting it, and doing everything I could to live a somewhat normal existence and not let the pain take over.

I also agonised over whether or not having children would exacerbate my fatigue and pain. For as long as I can remember, I desperately wanted to become a mum. At the orphanage, I would play with the dolls and babies, and being a mum was a dream I had always envisioned. Anyone who knew me could attest to the fact that my biggest life desire was to have my own children, so I was conflicted about the unknown impacts child-bearing would have on my body or if I should sacrifice having my own children to try and maintain my status quo.

The desire for motherhood was too big to ignore, and when my then husband assured me we would be okay, we decided to try – and it was okay. We adapted despite the extra pressure and pain (which is now a faint memory despite the ongoing issues females have post carry and post birth!).

I was fortunate to conceive immediately with both my

children. During my first pregnancy, from 12 weeks on, the hormonal changes and the growing pains caused terrible back and pelvic pain (pubic symphysis). Despite my baby being on the small side, my body struggled to carry the tiny load. I invested in stomach bands, back support, and support garments to help alleviate some of the pressure.

In addition to this, I had regular chiropractic and physiotherapy treatments; plus I continued doing Pilates for as long as possible to help strengthen my body. Often, I struggled with the associated pain, but I was so in love with being pregnant that it helped me change my perspective and cherish the experience. The fact that I was bringing new life into this world outweighed anything else. At 39 weeks, my firstborn, Ethan, decided it was his time to arrive.

Being familiar with pain, I laboured at home exceptionally well for ten hours. I was so calm that before I left the house, I was adamant that I needed to clean up and take the rubbish out, wanting to return to a clean house. The pain and the contractions were bearable; intense pain was nothing new, so I was extremely calm and reserved. My then husband, on the other hand, was a little more flustered and insisted that I get into the car, not wanting to risk it and have to facilitate me giving birth on the side of the road!

When I presented at the hospital, I was most likely already well-dilated. However, I was a little too reserved and calm for the midwives to take any real notice of me. Upon checking in, the midwives whispered that I had come in too early, but despite this

I was fortunate and thankful to be admitted. They provided me with two painkillers and told me to get some rest. At this point, they had not even examined me. Luckily, a midwife decided to come back and, seeing that the pain was escalating quickly, decided to examine me.

To her utter dismay, I was 10 centimetres dilated and was advised that I needed to give birth right away. The chaos surrounding this, especially getting my obstetrician into the delivery suite, was somewhat intense. We also discovered that my son was posterior (back to front), and because I was so far advanced, it was too late for any pain relief apart from gas. I admit that, by then, the pain was horrific.

The midwives and my obstetrician were phenomenal in guiding me through the birth, and my beautiful boy arrived in the early hours of the morning. Although I was still a little sore, the pelvic pain immediately subsided after giving birth. Oxytocin, the love hormone, flooded through my body, and I was in absolute love with my baby boy and absolute awe of the female body's capabilities. It was at this point that I discovered a new-found respect for my body and the strength that comes with giving birth to new life. It gave me a new perspective on my body's amazing (hidden) abilities.

Giving birth to my firstborn, Ethan James Richards, was a pivotal moment for me in understanding what my own entry into the world might have looked like and what I may have looked like as a baby. It was a beautiful insight for my mum and family as well. The whole birth process allowed me to uphold my birth mother in a way I never knew I could. It highlighted the pain she must have endured carrying two babies for nine months, only to have to give them up for adoption.

Ethan's birth allowed me to start to change the narrative about my entry into the world and the story I had created about being unloved and rejected. It made me realise that, at the young age of 16, my birth mum really had no choice but to give me up for adoption. In actual fact, she was forced to sign a statutory declaration relinquishing all responsibility and rights over both her children. Being an orphan herself, she had no other option.

Ethan's birth also allowed me to witness the love of the mother's heart. It gave me insight into the heartache my birth mum must have endured, if not immediately at 16, then perhaps later in her life. For the first time, I could empathise and feel what it would have been like to stand in her shoes and live a life where she had no choice, where there was no discussion.

A NEW CHAPTER, A SHIFTING STORY

After I gave birth to my son, my story started to shift. A new chapter was born, one where my birth mum made huge sacrifices to enable me to have the life I have today. With the arrival of Ethan came a new-found awareness of the person I was to become as a mum. With this new understanding, I was able to start the process of forgiveness and integrate my birth mum into my heart and my life. I would often sit and reflect on the person she might be, whether or not she would be alive today. At times,

I would experience immense sorrow knowing the tough life she probably had to live. Other times, I would envisage her living a fulfilling life.

My beautiful mum always offered to assist me with the search for my birth mum if I ever desired to find her, but I never had the urge to follow that path like some other adoptees do. I believe this was because I had a half-sister who was adopted alongside me, which allowed me to identify and connect with someone who possessed the same genetic make-up as me, who had the same blood pumping through her veins. This gave me a huge level of reassurance and connection, so I didn't feel so alone in this experience called life.

As we grew up together, my half-sister and I would sit and compare ourselves to each other. I would wonder what I inherited from my birth mother. We would intricately examine each aspect of our bodies to determine what we shared that was similar. It was our way of feeling connected during times when we often felt disconnected or didn't belong. Mind you, we share very little physical similarity, apart from our long fingers and the shape of our legs. Mostly, we are chalk and cheese, from the shape of our eyes, the shape of our nose, the colour of our skin, and even the composition of our hair.

They say there's an inseparable bond when it comes to twins, and I believe we had that type of bond. Often, we were slightly co-dependent. My younger sister relied heavily on me to be the parent and mother hen. It was how we survived in a world that, at times, still felt foreign to us.

Ethan was such a crucial part of my healing journey. He enabled me to experience and reclaim the childhood I never had. In nurturing my son, I was able to give myself the aspects of love and nurture that I missed during my infancy and connect with the younger aspect of myself, who was deprived of love. I found that each milestone Ethan reached was also a massive milestone for me in integrating the moments of growth I had never experienced nor had any stories of. Having Ethan was one of the biggest gifts in my healing journey and in instilling new life within me.

PAIN, HEARTACHE, AND NEW LIFE

In September 2016, I was blessed once again with the birth of my beautiful daughter, Zoe. Zoe means 'life', and boy was she a whirlwind of life in every way. She was wild, defiant, and strong as soon as she entered the world, and she taught me those principles. Even before she entered the world, she was defiant, rebellious, and did things her way.

Carrying Zoe was an ordeal. Many times during my pregnancy, I was conflicted because I should have been in love and excited about being pregnant, but the pain overrode a lot of the love and bliss. Throughout my first pregnancy, I had experienced some pubic symphysis and pelvic instability, but with the second the pain was immeasurable. I knew how to manage and deal with back pain, but pelvic instability and feeling like my pelvis was going to shatter underneath me was something I couldn't prepare for and had trouble reconciling while also trying to work, be a mum, be a partner, act joyous, and all the things in between.

From 30 weeks, I spent most days at home with my son, either lying down or lying in the bath, trying to get whatever natural pain relief I could. At 31 weeks, my OB told me my daughter was already engaged and to prepare to give birth soon. However, she ended up sitting there happily until 39 weeks. In the last trimester, I was so angry at the reality of this pregnancy and my daughter's stubbornness around not entering the world… or, more accurately, entering the world on her terms and not mine.

I have since asked her forgiveness, by the way, but I know now that the feeling is totally understandable! By 39 weeks, the pelvic pain was so overwhelming that I felt like my bones were breaking and there was a bowling ball between my legs. Unsurprisingly, scans post birth showed crack fractures in my pelvis.

At 39 weeks, I asked my OB to induce me. My stoic exterior made it look like I was somewhat at ease, but the pain was horrific. Upon examination, he realised that I was already 3 cm dilated and booked me in that afternoon to be induced. Ethan had been a tiny baby, weighing around 2.8 kg. Zoe, on the other hand, was 3.5 kg, and she wasn't only engaged but was sitting so low that when the OB broke my waters, he had a good chuckle because he had also cut her hair! My second labour was hard and fast, the pelvic pain so horrific I had trouble differentiating between labour pain and pubic pain. I couldn't feel anything apart from my pelvis throbbing. My only reassurance was that I knew that I could birth naturally, and the midwife was amazing in reassuring me throughout, helping me trust my body and be courageous while bringing new life into the world.

With the use of breathing techniques, meditation, and essential oils, I delivered Zoe in less than one hour and with literally two pushes. It was so rapid that my body went into shock, but the feeling of love, bliss, and elation finally surfaced! After an injection to comfort my body, I was able to focus on the joy of my new baby, studying every little detail of her face and her body. She was divine. A contrast to my son in her colouring and personality. I knew that I had a wild child on my hands – her arrival reinforced that in every way. I also knew that Zoe would be my last baby. Considering the extreme impact that carrying babies has on my body, my OB urged me not to have any more, and I agreed.

Similar to the birth of my firstborn, I was hoping that the pubic symphysis pain and pelvic pain would subside once my daughter was out. A small portion did fade, providing me with some relief, but the rest remained. Despite the pain and disappointment, the post-birth oxytocin produced by my body during the first few months following Zoe's birth kept me in a love bubble, allowing me to connect with my daughter.

Most days, I felt like I was in survival mode, trying to balance the needs of a toddler while feeding a baby who guzzled milk like there was no tomorrow. I experienced mastitis a number of times with Zoe, something I had never experienced with Ethan. I was extremely fatigued and lost a lot of weight, as mums typically do when running around after a toddler, breastfeeding, and not having enough time to catch up on sleep, let alone eat. In my case, I was also dealing with rehabilitating my body and managing chronic pain.

It took me long, agonising eight months to be able to simply walk around the block without feeling like my pelvis would shatter or being in absolute pain. Pain specialists told me that in order to heal, I shouldn't walk, I shouldn't carry my baby if standing upright. I shouldn't push a pram, or a trolley. I shouldn't food shop or do the housework. To some mums, it might sound like a dream, and it is in the sense that it isn't realistic. It certainly wasn't my reality. The recovery took years, with intense treatment from chiropractors and physiotherapists helping me rehabilitate my body, my pelvis, and my pelvic floor, all while struggling with huge fatigue issues common with new mums, plus the existing fatigue and immune issues that had been present long before having children.

Most days, the pain didn't subside, but I pushed through for my kids. After all, I had a 4-year-old and a baby I needed to care for. I did my best, despite still struggling to get out of bed. My life experience had taught me to keep going through whatever hardship arose. Now that I had two children to love, this responsibility superseded any of my needs, and over time the pain intensified.

My back and pelvic pain started radiating in other areas of my body and deep into my bones and joints. It radiated in my feet, and just walking the mere distance from my bed to the toilet was crippling. Add to that the immense sleep deprivation from having a baby, plus the recovery from carrying her while entertaining a toddler, and some days I wondered how all this had become my constant reality. The pain was all-encompassing. It riddled every aspect of my body. It engulfed me. Waking up each morning was simply a reminder of the oppressiveness I had within me. The seconds, minutes, hours, and days were long. I lost sight of the future, yet it was all I could think about. Why would I want an existence like this? What sort of life is it to be riddled with pain, experiencing little joy? I had always been strong and optimistic, so why was I crumbling beneath the weight of my pain now? The pain became so insurmountable, so deafening, haunting me relentlessly. It was all-consuming, and I couldn't get a moment's peace.

A DOUBLE-EDGED DIAGNOSIS

In July 2017, a rheumatologist diagnosed me with fibromyalgia. Most people who receive a diagnosis feel a huge sense of relief in being somewhat validated and seen, of finally having an explanation as to why they've been experiencing the symptoms and the pain for years on end after so long with no answers. For most diagnoses, I believe that this would ring true. However, with fibromyalgia, a relatively unknown condition with little known about how people acquire it, it meant there were very few treatment options apart from the standard Western medicine response from rheumatologists and doctors.

Despite giving me what felt like an interminable sentence, there was absolutely no sense of compassion or empathy. There was no direction given on how to adjust to living with fibromyalgia, nor interest in looking at the cause of the chronic pain or how to reduce it so it didn't progress into something even more debilitating. I was simply given a list of different prescription drugs and medications to consume. Anyone who has experienced long-term chronic pain would be familiar with the options available to them.

There are options like targeted cortisone injections directed into the disc and facets, which are administered to reduce the inflammation around the surrounding area and hopefully relieve the pain. This is similar to an epidural and is done under imaging technology to avoid further injury to vertebral discs and nerve roots. I had two rounds of this, but there was little relief. There's also the option to burn off nerve endings to block the pain signals, but it's a high-risk procedure, and the nerve endings grow back, meaning the pain can and will likely return. Among other recommendations from the rheumatologist was the suggestion to use SSRIs, or antidepressants, to improve my mood.

Antidepressants are often used to alter and increase serotonin levels in the brain in order to reduce symptoms of depression and anxiety. In saying this, I specifically mentioned that I wasn't depressed and was simply struggling with living in pain – a very fine distinction but one that often isn't heard by practitioners. Often, pain sufferers are put under the same umbrella as those who are depressed. Other prescription medications that are often used to treat fibromyalgia are long-term high doses of anti-inflammatories and nerve blockers to block the transmission of pain.

The diagnosis and the treatment plan felt cold, as was the rheumatologist's approach. Alongside receiving numerous prescriptions, I was told, "Your life will most likely never be the same again. You need to give up any expectation of doing the things you were once able to do, like exercising, hiking, walking, and so on." Hearing this was the cream on top of a horrible cake. Then my appointment time was up, and I was left trying to process the diagnosis solo. As I walked out of her consulting suite, I felt empty, disconnected, and so disappointed in the lack of support and understanding.

The diagnosis came when Zoe was 6 months old. I was still breastfeeding, and maintaining this was my biggest priority – firstly because I knew I wouldn't give birth again and also because I wasn't ready to give up the chance to strengthen that maternal bond. I knew just how imperative it was at that stage of infancy. I loved breastfeeding, and I wanted to stop on my terms, not be forced to make a decision that didn't align with my wishes or that was made out of sheer desperation. I had done that enough in the past when (in an attempt to do anything to remove the pain) I had taken and experimented with so many different medications and drugs.

I didn't want to put an unknown concoction of chemicals in my body, not knowing what the long-term ramifications would be and not knowing what harm I had already done to my body. I had made decisions in the past about my health that involved using treatments that I knew were experimental. I made them because I felt helpless when no other answers seemed available to me. I didn't want to be in that position again.

A SERIES OF PIVOTAL MOMENTS

At one point in my journey, I was accepted into a pain clinic. I had high hopes and expectations. The doctor was baffled by what could be causing all the pain. In looking at my history, my treatment, and my scans, including X-rays and MRIs, he proposed that the cause of pain may be due to an infection within my disc and facets. He mentioned that a study had recently been published that proposed that the occurrence of certain pain *could* be from an infection directly within the spine.

While he didn't have a lot of literature around this, he recommended that I take a low dose of antibiotics for three months to see if this would assist in reducing the pain. I had prior knowledge around the use of antibiotics and its impact on the gut microbiome – that is, the natural habitat of good and bad bacteria within the gut. Antibiotics, especially with long-term use, can have several negative effects, contributing to subsequent issues with the gut, the immune system, and cognition.[5]

A healthy functioning microbiome plays a huge role in our overall health and wellbeing. Despite having this awareness and knowing that the long-term use of antibiotics could have a detrimental effect on my overall health and wellbeing, I went against my intuition. I took them as a last resort, a 'just in case this works and eliminates the pain' desperate decision, as I had nearly lost all hope. I only lasted six weeks, as I started to experience excruciating pain in my stomach.

This experience was a pivotal moment for me because it made me realise that going against your intuition can have consequences, and for me it now meant having to heal the damage caused to my gut while still addressing the original pain. For too many years, I had made decisions about my health in desperation, feeling like I had little option or control.

Rather than feeling powerless, it was time to take charge and commit to researching and doing due diligence around what would be best for me, something that only each individual can know for themself. With this clearer resolve in my heart, I knew that I didn't want to venture down the path of taking prescription medications because I could easily become reliant on them without actually fixing the root problem. I also knew that, even though the pain challenged my mental health and I sometimes struggled mentally and emotionally, I fundamentally wasn't depressed. I can only thank my studies in psychology for this knowledge and awareness.

In addition, I had a sudden clarity and realisation that my body was omitting pain for a reason, so if I could identify why, then I could reduce the pain. Taking medicine (which without a doubt can be beneficial and at times does serve a purpose) would hinder me in trying to unravel the layers of pain. If I were using nerve blockers, then how would my brain communicate and tell me I was in pain? Would I end up doing more damage to myself in the long term? And despite the numerous conversations around inflammation, why wasn't there ever any talk about what could have been contributing to this?

Walking out of the pain clinic's consulting suite that day with such a pure perspective and awareness was another pivotal moment in my life. I would never again rely on a system that didn't enable me to be empowered within myself and my body without giving me options, alternatives, choices. My rebel side (still rumbling away from conforming to rigid systems for years) resurfaced, and I resolved to identify the cause of my pain and, more importantly, what my body was telling me.

The year 2017 was one of my most challenging, but it was also a crucial turning point. Awareness of fibromyalgia was starting to emerge among medical practitioners, but many were still sceptical, pronouncing it to be a ghost condition or psychosomatic. Some would even project their opinions and views onto me and tell me that it was not real, yet for someone who was living with chronic, pervasive pain, I knew it to be very real.

In 2017, I sat in my lounge room, tears streaming down my face as I contemplated what it would look like if I ended my life. I looked at what I had and knew there could be more to my life than my current existence. I reflected on my kids and most definitely did not want them to be without a mum, nor did I want them to know the grief associated with the loss of a parent; that would be unthinkably unfair.

I contacted numerous suicide helplines, which metaphorically helped me get off the edge of my ledge – that is, my thoughts. My studies surrounding psychology were a saving grace, too. During my postgrad studies, I learnt that when patients display and show signs of helplessness and hopelessness around the future, when they can't envisage a future, it's a primary indicator of feeling suicidal. However, I knew that in my case it was because of my pain.

I knew there had to be change, so, as I contemplated leaving this world, I decided instead to make a pact with God. I had been raised in a Christian environment, but I had deviated from the traditional church doctrine over the years. During my late teens and early 20s, I struggled with elements of religion, especially those aspects that were riddled with hypocrisy and judgement of others. I felt that I and many others were being shamed and ostracised for decisions we made when we didn't know better, and too many of us have carried that shame our entire lives.

To me, faith is a totally different thing from religion. I knew that there was a greater force and existence beyond me, so I made an agreement that if this greater force (God, universe, whoever you like to reference) would assist me and guide me to obtain the answers I needed to break through the barriers of pain, then I would commit to assisting others facing similar challenges. I would make it my life's mission to help others through their chronic pain journey.

Listening to the prognosis from those specialists left little room for hope. It could have easily led to my demise and the end of my life, as I know it does for so many. It can feel like a life sentence that can be so restrictive and debilitating. Yet it was also like a beacon, tuning me into a different message, one coming from within. I decided not to allow the diagnosis to be the end; rather, it was the beginning. While it took every ounce of courage for me to continue to live with the presence of pain every day, I made a conscious decision to no longer fight the pain, create resistance, or be at war with it. Instead, I started uncovering and discovering the layers of my pain, which I realised were many.

This was such a crucial period in my life and the start of my healing journey.

Understanding my responsibility in all of this was the first real catalyst for change. I could sense the depths of how the cycle of trauma manifests in the physical body. I knew that I had a responsibility not only to my children but also to myself to start to create change, to want better, to search for better, to discover new alternatives, to stop feeling sorry for myself, to find the inner depths of who I was, to find joy despite the pain.

I wanted to rewrite my story. I didn't want my time on Earth to be without purpose. I wanted to look in the mirror and know that the person looking back at me had done everything in her power to create the life she was here to live. I wanted to look at her, not with disdain and pity but with love. I wanted to like the person within me.

Along the way, there were challenges, hardships, tears, frustration, anger – bucketloads, in fact. But as I started to let go of so much baggage, trauma, expectations of self, loss and grief, and stored emotions, it all gave way for other things to enter. I started to see things differently; I started to believe in myself, and my world started to change.

Atticus, a beautiful poet, once wrote, "Sometimes to find the way, we must have first lost the way." It was now time not to find but to reclaim my way.

BE YOUR OWN MEDICAL ADVOCATE

Let me reveal a misconception. Most people assume I've always been the free-spirited hippy I often appear to be today, but throughout my 20s I was far from it. I was your typical modern 20-year-old; I worked hard, played hard, and enjoyed drinking, smoking, and partying. I was health conscious, but I deviated from this path on the weekends in favour of fun in any shape or form.

Unfortunately, my body had other plans, and you could say if it weren't for the chronic pain, fatigue, and endless gut issues, I would likely still be a Type A personality mover and shaker, trying to prove to the world that I had my shit together in an attempt to be accepted and affirmed.

Some people are forced to listen to their body's sudden screams; others experience more of a slow burn. What began as whispery feelings of burnout and fatigue in my mid- to late-20s became louder and louder until my body was screaming and I had no choice but to make considerable changes.

Over more than a decade, I researched and dabbled in many diverse modalities, from the more traditional and well-known that are generally more aligned with Western medicine to unconventional modalities that focus more on healing from the inside out.

As I investigated, I noticed numerous themes. As patients, we place so much subliminal pressure on external people to fix us, to cure us. When this doesn't happen, we're awash with disappointment and disillusionment, sometimes at the 'expert', sometimes at our own bodies. We place so much faith and hope into a single practitioner, thinking our healing comes from someone else's knowledge they've gained from studying anatomy. Most of us don't realise it's not the 'expert' that actually heals us.

We need to take a step back to see the bigger picture. The professional may give us their expertise, guidance, and medicine, but this is only effective when working in conjunction with your body to heal *itself*. The healing comes from within, by some internal trigger or change that tells your body it needs to readjust or let go.

Different practitioners will guide you in different areas of the body, and sometimes you'll need to build a team of experts that align with your values and beliefs. The most alarming realisation is that not all practitioners will have your best interests in mind; many won't know how to treat chronic pain nor understand the somatic elements of how trauma can cause physical pain and how that pain can cause further trauma.

Many practitioners will overtax and over-burn your nervous system; some might even cause more damage than good. It's all a learning curve, often a very steep one, especially when we put these practitioners on a pedestal and expect them to fix us.

You must be your own advocate.

No one, not one single practitioner, will know what you need better than you. But over the years, we've lost our ability to connect to our internal guidance system, which is why we put so much pressure on our medical system to tell us what's wrong.

We haven't been taught how to trust our body or pick up on all the telltale signs that something may not be right internally or the different cues that tell us action is needed. We haven't been taught that fatigue isn't normal, aches and pains without reason aren't normal, feeling lacklustre and without joy isn't something we should accept as the daily norm, pushing and overworking our bodies and minds can actually overtax and burn out the nervous system, and anxiety doesn't mean we're crazy.

We learn to ignore these signs, to suppress them. I had numerous occasions when I silenced myself and didn't speak up, times when things didn't make sense, and I was gaslit or made to think I was a little mad.

Here are some of those instances:

- When I used to experience excruciating abdominal pain (from a very early age and up until my teenage years), I searched for answers, but despite having a gastroscopy and colonoscopy, they couldn't determine what was wrong, so they told me to take an anti-reflux drug, even though I didn't have reflux.

    I trusted them and took the medication, even though the recommendation didn't make sense and even though I kept experiencing gut issues. I was then told by a different gastroenterologist to get off the drug as soon as possible because the body can become dependent upon it. It wasn't until I started seeing naturopaths and kinesiologists and removed inflammatory foods that were contributing to my gut dysbiosis that my stomach pains finally subsided. Diet

and stress were huge contributing factors and still are to this day!
- When I saw a physiotherapist to treat my chronic pain, and she told me to stress less and work less. Or when I saw a different physiotherapist who told me that my pain wasn't real and was purely psychosomatic, but I knew it was more than a figment of my imagination. It was much more.
- When I saw an exercise physiologist and told him of certain exercises I couldn't do because it would trigger my lower back pain and the weakness that resided there, he dismissed this, telling me to trust him, and I ended up with considerable lower back pain that rendered me unable to walk and move properly for a month.
- When I took antidepressants, even though I wasn't depressed, and it didn't feel like the right decision for me and my body. I was so desperate for something to shift my pain, but the medication left me feeling disorientated, confused, and anxious as hell.

There are also times when I did trust myself, and I did speak up:
- When I said no to the antidepressant and the antispasmodic drugs my specialist wanted me to try out in an attempt to reduce the pain.
- When I said yes to taking prescription drugs to assist with vertigo.
- When I experienced ongoing pain in my left ovary, and

pelvic and internal scans showed nothing, I raised my voice and asked for further investigation. It turned out to be endometriosis.

Many of us dismiss these signals and signs, thinking that doctors and other practitioners always know what's best for us when often that's not the case. Yes, they can share their expertise and light on what they think may help us (may being the operative word), but because each body is different and each body responds differently to treatments and drugs, we as individuals must be aware of this and listen to how our body responds to treatment. We also must ensure that whatever treatment we expose ourselves to aligns with our inherent values around how we want to treat ourselves and our body.

One of the biggest issues behind our reliance on the mainstream medical fraternity is that our connection to self, our intuition, has been so heavily influenced by numerous factors that cause us to disconnect and distrust ourselves. Trauma has the same effect and causes polarity within our body. We lose understanding and trust in ourselves.

Part of my journey has been rediscovering all this knowledge and understanding the true impact of our upbringing and how this can manifest in our body and influence how we heal. We are a product of our environment, our experiences, our parents' upbringing, our teachers, our community, our traumas, and so on and so forth. All of these factors influence our thoughts, our beliefs, our perceptions, and can define the person we become if we're not aware of the role they play and if we don't continue to question how well they serve us as we grow and learn.

Often, when we come to this realisation, it's very easy to project blame on all those who have contributed to the not-so-positive aspects of ourselves. We as humans love to shift blame, love to project, love to be void of responsibility.

For years, I was in victim mode, not consciously but subconsciously. I was born into the sadness and grief of the world. This was my reality, so a lot of my existence became trying to justify the actions of other people, especially my birth mother.

My teenage years reinforced this victim perspective. I questioned why bad things happened and why they kept happening to me. Chronic pain was my constant reminder of how difficult life was for me, and it wasn't until I began to understand how trauma can impact the human body (from a physical and energetic perspective), creating an imbalance, that I could see the connection – my trauma was presenting in my body as dysfunction and disease.

While it's really easy to project blame when we look back, in actual fact, no one is to blame for the person we are today. We are a by-product of our environment. This is true for every single person on Earth, regardless of their location or the circumstances they're born into. This means that each different generation has very different personal experiences that will develop into different beliefs, opinions, reactions, and schools of thought, which influence the people they become. Understanding these significant factors in an individual's upbringing is the most powerful step in empowering ourselves to heal and shape our future free of pain.

HUMAN EMOTION: LAYERS OF GRIEF AND HOPE

If I thought I had endured enough throughout my life, it was nothing compared to the events to come. Like a rocket exploding and propelling me so far forward, the sudden passing of my beloved brother Ton at the young age of 49 blasted me out of my current reality.

We had been in the throes of planning his 50th birthday celebrations in December of 2018 when he had a heart attack, and, like a nightmare, we were suddenly planning his funeral instead. Nothing ever prepares you for the call that tells you your brother didn't make it. Yet here I was, at the end of another seemingly ordinary day, feeding Zoe to get her to sleep, when I received the dreaded call from my sister. The week thereafter was a whirlwind.

We were all in fight-or-flight mode, trying to get through the logistics while also trying to support one another. Our grief was put on hold for a short while as we managed the funeral and upheld each other through the frustration, anger, hurt, pain, disbelief, grief, and loss while trying to process what had happened and how a brother could have passed. We put all our feelings and pain aside, rallying together as a family to celebrate his life.

Afterwards, I crashed and burnt. My nervous system was so burnt out from the stress of it all that it took me weeks to recover and comprehend the new reality. My experiences studying psychology and my one unit studying loss and grief (or as my mum and I used to call it, 'loss and groff') meant that I had an awareness of the loss and grief cycle. My mum, who is also a family therapist, had this awareness as well, and together we had in-depth discussions about the different types of loss we endure as humans. However, experiencing it firsthand was a totally different thing. Loss ripples through your body with such intensity and physical heartache that it's like a physical affliction.

Despite the pain of Tony's passing, it brought us closer together as a family. It helped us appreciate each other more, reassess our priorities, and stop sweating the small stuff. While we could have all been trapped within the loss and grief of it all, we made a conscious decision to celebrate his life and our lives every day.

Grief affects people differently. It isn't only the loss that you need to come to terms with but also all the different scenarios and the 'what ifs' as you try to rationalise and question how it could have occurred and how and if it could have been prevented. For my parents, it challenged every notion they had about life's natural cycle and the idea that no parent should ever have to bury their child. For Tony's wife and kids, the grief was magnified, as they endured such an enormous personal loss. For Tony's siblings, it was painful proof of how quickly life can be taken away, shaking the foundations of everything once believed in.

It was then that I started to discover for myself the impact of stagnant emotions. When I held on to the loss and grief associated with not only Tony's passing but also the loss and grief connected to numerous aspects of my life, I realised firsthand that the emotions were compounding within my body, manifesting in my joints and muscles as fibromyalgia pain.

This experience taught me to become really aware of my body and to witness the correlation between emotions that are not 'in flow' (or in motion) becoming trapped and stagnant. This build-up of emotions creates pressure, which then affects the body, physically manifesting as inflammation, aches, and pains.

The more I explored this link, the clearer it became. When I had an emotional release, I felt the pain release within my physical body as well. As I allowed the tears to flow, I felt a huge sense of physical pressure being lifted, as if the accumulation of trapped emotions was suddenly being set free on a tangible scale. It was like a tightly sealed vacuum breaking open for the first time, the air releasing at speed.

Along with the relief, I now understood the strength in honouring our emotions by allowing them to be expressed, as opposed to holding on to them tightly and never releasing them, a strategy the majority of the world's population has been taught as a coping mechanism.

There's so much strength in knowing that we don't need to have it together, that it's strong to be authentic and vulnerable. To this day, I'm often reminded of Tony through photos or conversations, and instead of focusing on our loss and the fact that he's not here, I focus on his spirit, his personality, the legacy he left behind, and how he would want us to live our lives – and that is with impact.

WHEN IT RAINS…

If having a loved one pass away wasn't enough, the challenges of the following year, 2019, continued to turn my world upside down. Firstly, my role in the company where I had worked for over a decade became redundant. Suddenly, I was thrown into an identity crisis trying to figure out who I was without this role. For years, I had associated myself with that company and that role. I had grown and evolved, undertaken numerous roles, developed numerous relationships and friendships, and had two children along the way. I had spent a significant portion of my life there, and now I was suddenly unemployed. What the redundancy did provide me with was the time to determine what I wanted. In retrospect, it was divine timing ready for the next bombshell to hit me.

Fast-forward two months, and an enormous personal and family test arrived: the breakup of my marriage. While you might be anticipating that I need to delve into the personal aspects of the breakup, it's a personal choice not to because doing so wouldn't be beneficial for me, nor anyone reading this. As I grow, experience, and witness more and more, I've come to understand that, as individuals, our interpretation of any reality is based upon our own subjective experiences, so regardless of my perception of the experience, it will ultimately differ from another's.

No two people can experience the same reality, so until we can put ourselves in the other person's shoes, we really should not (and cannot) judge another. With this in mind, I choose not to delve into the intricacies of my marriage but rather focus on the fact that I was married for a decade, and that part of my life brought me much happiness, many amazing experiences, and two beautiful children. I will, however, offer some explanation.

I met my ex-husband in my mid-20s. We were both young and vivacious, without a care in the world. We both worked and played hard. We married at 28. We saved hard and created a wonderful life together. We supported each other through the pressures of adult life. We created memories, shared experiences, and had two kids together. But after 15 years together, we grew apart. We fundamentally became two very different people who wanted very different things, and despite all the conversations, all the healing, all the effort, we realised it was over.

We were no longer in a capacity where we could uphold or bring out the best in each other. Despite how excruciatingly hard it was to have these conversations, we knew it would be even harder to live a life where we were unhappy, trying to raise two kids within this environment. It didn't mean there wasn't a lot of heartache over what we were losing – there was – along with mourning the loss of any future dreams together. There was so much loss and heartache.

It hit me like a freight train; some moments, I would almost collapse, as my heart literally felt like it was breaking. I had to manage quite a few panic attacks as I tried to untangle how on

Earth I was going to get through the next few months while caring for the kids' needs, especially emotionally. The loss and the sadness that came with my marriage breakup were immense, taking me months and months to process.

However, instead of shunning the pain and pretending it didn't exist, for the first time in my life, I gave it space to be heard, to be recognised. I started to realise that the intricate parts of me were yearning to be heard, and ignoring them wouldn't be beneficial in any way. Despite wanting to bury my head in the sand and ignore what was happening (note: my previous default), I knew that this was an opportunity for me to not default to victim mode and to instead approach the situation with a maturity I may not have exhibited before. In a way, I was forced to grow up, especially with two kids I also had to emotionally uphold and care for.

I was forced to face my problems head-on. I made some apt decisions that gave me the time and space to focus on my family. I was also studying, so I made the prompt decision to defer university so I could focus solely on mourning and surviving. Most days, I just put one foot in front of the other and only did what I could to survive. For many days, this was watching Netflix to disconnect from the whirlwind of thoughts and emotions that hounded me.

Other days, it was mustering up the courage to venture outside with tear-stained eyes and a heaviness that I thought would never leave me. But this time, I was trusting my past experiences, which were telling me that I just needed to sit within the emotional pain and allow it to surface and emerge however it needed to. Keeping it trapped would mean the fibromyalgia and physical pain would rear itself again, and this was something I couldn't afford. So, I made a conscious decision to go inward, to focus solely on me and my two kids. On the days I could emerge, I would. On the days I couldn't, I wouldn't.

EMBRACING A NEW BEGINNING

One day, out of nowhere, something magical happened. The oppressiveness started to shift; the darkness started to lift. As I woke that morning, for the first time in weeks, the sound of the birds chirping made me smile. How something so minute and simple could elicit a change within me was incredible, and I felt a glimmer of hope. I started to sense the beauty of the world again, something I thought may never return. That little spark grew bigger, and I could focus on bringing in the things that weren't so heavy, the things that felt lighter. It was the peace after the storm, and even though the pain was still there, it no longer felt like a sword through my heart. I could almost place it aside for short periods so I could function. I knew it was all going to be okay. More importantly, this time around, I knew I didn't have to do it alone. My default had always been to believe that I had to do it alone, to pretend and create a facade that everything was okay, even though everything wasn't. I had so many people reach out to me with love and support.

The university I was attending (I was studying postgrad in psychotherapy) gifted me free sessions to see a counsellor. She was a lot older and wiser than me and gave me so much practical advice that mostly involved placing one foot in front of the other. She taught me how to be more present in my body, to validate all the myriad of emotions I was experiencing, and to give voice to them. She allowed me to be heard, to be felt, and to be seen.

The wonderful thing about sharing and expressing your emotions is that it allows you to share the weight and burden from your physical body.

This emotional release makes space for other things to come in lieu of them, but we aren't taught this in any educational setting. Often, relationships come with such volatile emotions, which we're programmed to harbour and hold on to in order to get through the pain and angst. Having someone objective to confide in meant that I shifted these emotions more quickly and gained the clarity I needed to make big life decisions that benefitted me and my kids. There was no spite involved; I simply did what would serve all of us best.

I also recognised that I needed to align myself with women who not only had my best interests at heart but who could also draw up the strength within me and remind me not to deviate too far from my values and my path. It was also the prime opportunity to rediscover what these key values were after a lifetime of sharing them with others.

It was like I was being stripped back to my core, without my corporate identity to fall back on or my identity as a wife or partner. It was time to call up my own personal power in order to do what I needed to do, to be able to speak up for myself, and to ultimately do the scary things as a single parent. Funnily enough, the people I was more attracted to reminded me what was important: my health, my wellbeing and my kids' wellbeing, which also meant their dad's wellbeing. It wasn't about revenge and malice; it was about peace, which meant not harbouring anything that didn't benefit or serve us, plus maintaining love.

Often, when big life changes occur, whether that's the death of a loved one, the death of a relationship, or the death of a job, we're so thick within it that we can't see beyond the emotions, the pain, and the hurt. The cloudiness seems oppressive and heavy; the fears seem to loom, and the anxiety starts to creep in. This is all normal, but it's important to recognise that, during these times, we need to excuse ourselves, give compassion to ourselves for experiencing these emotions, not judge ourselves, and not seek to inflict pain and or pass judgement on others, for this too is a defence mechanism.

THE POWER OF RISING ABOVE VICTIMHOOD

Pain, whether it be emotional pain, physical pain, or even mental pain and anguish, can skew our ability to see, feel or perceive things clearly. After living with chronic pain for a decade, **I was living proof of how much pain can restrict and influence your perception and how it can cause you to default into victim mode and keep you trapped.**

Despite the moments when I still wanted to feel like the victim, I learnt not to stew on my emotions or act on them; instead, I learnt to process them first. I also learnt not to default to the victim mentality or the poor me syndrome. I was adamant about shifting this; I couldn't carry this heavy mentality any longer. Please note that there wasn't an instant solution. This is most definitely a work in progress, and at times I get it wrong and tantrum, but, as life goes on, I'm more likely to exhibit emotional maturity than fall prey to old behaviours and mindsets that keep me limited and stuck.

After a five-month break from working, I decided to return to the workforce for numerous reasons. However, I had my reservations, especially around the level of physical investment required for me to not only work but also to maintain my health while selling the family home, caring for two kids, and recovering from a lot of stress and trauma. Despite these concerns, I needed to focus my energy on something apart from being a single mum. I needed purpose and to prove to myself that I had the strength and capability to do the things I once did. This time though, I knew how important it was not to hide my situation; I knew that would only compound the stress of it. Therefore, I was extremely transparent in each job I applied for, advising them that I was going through a separation and that if my kids needed me, I would literally have to drop and run.

I no longer wanted to hide in shame. I needed support, and, for that to occur, I needed to be courageous and ask for it. Instead of being ostracised and judged, my new boss reassured me and shared her own story of being a divorcee. I also told my managing director, an amazing man who led with empathy.

I remember a distinct conversation we had about people often forgetting that fancy job titles don't stop you from being human. After I showed vulnerability and transparency, along with my passion, he valued me even more. He actively practised an open-door policy, and I approached him many times on different levels to work out how to accommodate any issues so I could still work effectively.

In my previous role, I would have shaken in my boots at the thought of ever crying and being vulnerable in front of the Managing Director, afraid it would reveal that I, in fact, didn't have it all together. It was time to break some of these stigmas for myself, stop hiding in self-proclaimed shame and instead allow others to support me. After all the recent loss and grief, I was adamant about breaking down and dismantling some of the masks and personas I had created over the years for fear of being rejected.

We often forget that people, regardless of roles, positions, and stereotypes, are human, and ultimately, as humans, we all want to be seen and heard. When we allow ourselves to be vulnerable, when we lead with our heart, the majority of people in our lives will respond with love, compassion, and support, but if you don't allow it to happen and if you close yourself to the world, you also close yourself to this type of support.

At a time when I most certainly questioned the intent and behaviour of men and was likely to bundle all men into vast stereotypes that weren't true, I was instead reminded of their strength and kindness. When I could have easily become a bitter and twisted female and, in turn, spiteful and resentful, I made a conscious effort to ensure that hate and anger didn't manifest into something bigger because then hate wins, and we as individuals lose.

Hurt and heartache often make us close ourselves off to further hurt. This means shutting people out and closing off our hearts for protection. We also try to rationalise the heartache and the pain, looking for a reason for it. If we don't learn to take full responsibility for our part, we often project blame towards others for creating the hurt and pain. This can mean sometimes tarring the gender that has hurt us as being unjust or behaving badly, which is extremely easy to do when history has shown generations of females being oppressed for patriarchal gain.

At a time when I could have easily categorised all men as arseholes, the men who showed up in my life exuded kindness and were my reminder not to assign labels. It reminded me that men, too, have countless experiences, good and bad, that influence the people they are today. This was my lesson not to subscribe any longer to victimising myself or pitying myself. This was my time to rise beyond that and to draw strength and courage from all different avenues, both externally and internally. It was time to recognise all the amazing resources available to me.

As time passed, I felt less grief and more snippets of joy and happiness. I realised that at the mere age of 39, my entire life was still ahead of me. Many of us are faced with a mid-life crisis between 40 and 50 years of age, when we have some sort of existential test and start contemplating our existence on Earth. We question what the purpose of life is and if it's really just working, parenting, and doing the mundane things. For me, this crisis or awareness was an awakening. In a way, it was forced upon me, but instead of allowing myself to be trapped by my past, I had a new awareness that celebrated everything that had got me to that point, all my experiences and achievements, good and bad. I no longer wanted to be defined by what I considered negative or traumatic. I wanted to tear down the strongholds. I wanted something better for myself, and I knew that now was the moment to start creating it.

I decided to follow the path of self-discovery, to find all the aspects of myself I had lost over the years, all those aspects that I had disregarded. The aspects I had cut off that I didn't think had a time or place, the ones that I sacrificed or were actually a part of me but, out of fear of being rejected and not being enough, I rejected. I wanted to find all these aspects of myself again and rediscover who I truly was.

It was my time to be rebirthed, and I wanted to understand who this person was that had been waiting within, who had experienced so much loss and grief. I wanted to ask her to step up, to speak up, to stop waiting or even asking for permission, to stop needing to be affirmed by others. I wanted to discover her deepest desires as her own individual person, not as a mum, wife, partner, daughter, friend, or colleague. I no longer wanted to be defined.

I had the deepest urge to follow my heart, my soul, to no longer be repressed, to no longer be versions of me that I had created in order to fit in, or versions of me that weren't congruent with who I truly was. I was sick of wearing the masks, or needing to seek approval, sick of hiding myself for fear of judgement. My inner soul was desperate to emerge and to be heard and seen, away from the pain that I had carried within me for so long. This was my time.

Welcome to the journey of true self-discovery and unleashing the absolute true potential within, regardless of the perception of what may be holding you back.

Part 3

UNRAVELLING CHRONIC PAIN

From years of my own experience living with pain, researching, studying, learning, and working with clients, I've discovered many recurring themes behind the causes of chronic pain and the individual challenges of living and dealing with it. It can be different for everyone; however, as a guide, I've collated the following material and literature to help people with chronic pain guide themselves through healing their own trauma and challenges so we can start to flip the notion and the belief that we are powerless.

PAIN IS NOT THE ENEMY

Many of us with chronic pain and autoimmune conditions believe we're broken and need to be fixed. This narrative is often fed to us via practitioners, mass marketing, and even those close to us. For the majority of my life, I believed there was something fundamentally wrong with me and that I needed to be fixed. I believed that the pain housed within my body was the issue, but this way of thinking isn't conducive to enabling the body to heal, nor guiding our mental, emotional, or physical health and recovery. Instead of perceiving pain to be the enemy, I want people to 'rediscover' that pain is our body's way of expressing and communicating with us.

Pain is an ally (not an enemy) and can be the catalyst for making considerable changes in our lives if we allow it.

Although pain can limit us, it can also be the gift that allows us to break through pre-existing limitations that we hold over ourselves. Many of us don't realise that we have the choice to either live with continual suffering (which, from years of personal experience, I can tell you totally sucks) or we can make a conscious choice to create change and live at our absolute full potential within the body we were gifted. *But how?* I hear you ask.

To create this shift, you will need to unravel many old principles that most of us have been operating blindly under for all our lives. By objectively re-evaluating our knowledge of them, we can start to realign to our ancient truths and wisdom, the wisdom that our ancestors and their ancestors carried within them. We can start to take this wisdom and integrate it into our lives and way of living, to be more mindful, to be more present, to be more connected within ourselves and our bodies, as opposed to thinking and believing that we have no control over what occurs within our body or pain we experience.

At first, you may want to resist some of what I present here and even what your inner voice is telling you. Comments like, *You don't understand. I've tried everything. It's not me… it's everyone else.* I too resisted for many years, but I know that living in chronic pain and avoiding yourself is harder than not doing the work. The work won't be easy. Confronting your past, your experiences, the old beliefs you want to cling to and dismantling heavy mindsets is without a doubt hard and painful, which is why so many people don't do it, but this is the way forward to lift your pain. Unbeknownst to most, however, is that our baggage is what contributes to keeping us trapped within our physical pain. We carry it every day, wondering why we have this weight on our shoulders that we can't identify.

The concepts within this part of the book will set the background and context for attitudes and treatment of pain over the decades. It will show you a new perspective on how and why you've reached the point of pain you're at today. If you're reading this book, I know that you desire to create change for yourself. I hope this book is the catalyst for you opening yourself to new possibilities and embracing a new way of thinking, believing, and living. I hope you will be open to unravelling the areas that are contributing to your pain as you let this new reality show you a lighter way.

LOVING OUR HUMAN DESIGN

Let's begin by appreciating the uniqueness of the human experience and, importantly, our human form. We are born to enjoy a human body and mind that has been expertly designed over many thousands of years, designed so we can live a thriving, intelligent, spiritual, and emotional life.

Over the ages, we have evolved and developed to rely on technological advancements to make our lives easier and more comfortable; human 'survival' has never been more successful than it is right now. We live in a technological culture that has become disconnected from many aspects of our 'natural' selves, meaning we rely on our human instincts less and less. As the need for manual work to survive has declined, we have filled our lives (days and minutes even) with more mental stimulation than ever.

While we're busy on our smartphones and searching the Internet for every little fact known to man, we're actually taking for granted the amazing tasks our body accomplishes instinctively each day to keep us alive. Our body performs countless sophisticated processes each moment of the day. Every single minute, our body sends blood pumping through our heart; it oxygenates our blood; it removes carbon dioxide; it creates energy; it removes toxins; it can even prevent the onset of disease, with certain enzymes constantly checking DNA strands for signs of disease and replacing damaged parts.[1]

In addition, our body has the incredible ability to rejuvenate itself. The skeletal system will fully regenerate itself approximately eight times over an average lifetime.[2] In fact, the average age of cells in the human body is 7–10 years, with some cells renewing every few days and others taking decades to renew.[3] We humans are dynamic and constantly evolving and regenerating. Our bodies instinctively do all of this work to keep us alive each and every day. Unless you've studied human anatomy or biology, or have been raised quite holistically to understand these intrinsic processes, the fact is, the majority of people's everyday awareness of human function is very limited and often overlooked. Most us (me included), assume that each day we'll be able to wake up refreshed every morning, eat when we're hungry (nowadays even when we're not), drink when we're thirsty, expel when our bodies tell us to, feed information to our brain, learn and study, work and exercise, and then afterwards we'll fall asleep each night and wake again to repeat the cycle.

We create assumptions that our body will continue to perform these tasks effortlessly each and every day without questioning this ability or considering how to support it. Even if you simply perceive your body to be the vessel that gets you from A to B, every vessel needs fuel, support, and maintenance. So, when we start to experience chronic pain, our disconnection from ourselves often means that we don't have the awareness or the intuitive connection with our body to know where to start looking for the answers or understand why the pain has appeared.

WESTERN MEDICINE: A SYMPTOMS-BASED APPROACH THAT LIMITS US

Many of us living in the Western world are incredibly privileged to have access to amazing healthcare and a vast array of specialists who provide different resources and treatments based upon each individual's needs. The majority of the medical system operates predominantly under the principles of Western medicine, which is commonly described as a symptom- or evidence-based approach.

The Western medicine model originated in the 19th century. Through scientific research and discoveries, it helped overcome many health challenges of the colonial period to do with infection and the spread of germs in dense populations. It was a turning point in improving living conditions for vast populations of people. For example, the early medical schools of Europe and America were a watershed in improving hygiene standards, which dramatically lowered infection rates (and associated fatalities), particularly in situations such as army field hospitals treating injured soldiers and in childbirth where the mother often died from infection picked up during labour.[4]

As more lives were being saved in this period of expansion, it's understandable that doctors were pretty impressed with their methods. As time went on, they gained more conviction in their methodology and treatment of disease. Doctors and scientists collected an endless catalogue of disease symptoms and data about how disease presents so this knowledge could be analysed, categorised, labelled, and carefully placed into alphabetical position in a medical reference book. Modern Western medicine has been adding to these categories, labels, and textbooks ever since, and, in many ways, we know more about the human body than ever before.

However, this method of medicine has created a dependence (or a narrow view) on diagnosing and treating illness only from a symptoms-based approach. It has created a medical system designed to treat acute disease stemming from a single physical cause that has been studied and catalogued previously. These principles – while expert and life-saving in so many ways – do not, in my experience, provide enough understanding or support to treat and manage chronic pain. In practical terms, a symptoms-based approach means that when an individual experiences a symptom or feels unwell, they'll go to the doctor to assess the symptom, make a diagnosis, and provide advice on how to treat and hopefully reduce the symptom, often with medication.

However, when the symptoms are more complex or can't be seen (only described), their cause becomes harder to identify; therefore, a diagnosis becomes unlikely. Looking at a patient's symptoms solely from a symptoms-based viewpoint, especially when the patient's ailments are invisible to the naked eye and don't show up in medical screening and pathological tests, can leave the patient at a loss. The ambiguity and the lack of diagnosis can result in a patient becoming more confused than they were when they first arrived at the appointment! The hope that they may have placed in the practitioner to explain their symptoms quickly diminishes. Although these symptoms may not be visible to the naked eye, they still limit the patient's ability to undertake day-to-day activities. Therefore, some sort of chronic dysfunction is present that needs to be heard and taken seriously.

As long as chronic pain doesn't fit into our medical society's accepted symptom categories (almost like it's in the too-hard basket), Western medicine will struggle to interpret the signals and messages *beyond* an individual's pain and will therefore struggle to offer any real solutions beyond a pill to mask the discomfort for a time. Increasingly, patients will need to look for alternatives that, I can assure you, are out there, and they often work well when integrated with Western medicine. For many patients who have lost hope in the system, lost hope that there are treatments and solutions available to them, lost hope in their body and even in themselves, *my* hope for all is that they rediscover their hope. Because there are, in actual fact, treatments and options available to them, but they require them to deviate from traditional medicine and adopt a more integrated approach to healing and treatment.

Understanding that there are both options available to us is where the biggest hurdle often lies. While I no longer rely wholly on the traditional methods of medicine we're so accustomed to here in Australia, I don't discount them either; I utilise what works for me. There simply needs to be a greater understanding around how numerous factors that fall outside traditional scientific methods are actually incredibly significant when looking at chronic pain case by case. Many effective methodologies originated long before conventional science. Unfortunately, the general attitude throughout society and the medical fraternity is that anything 'holistic' and not of the traditional scientific method is implausible.

Yet, to really treat and manage pain beyond the obvious physical level, we need to look at the function of the whole body – this includes brain and mind function and their effects on our nervous system – and only then can we begin to decipher how and why the pain has originated for us in the first place. Once you start exploring the broader view of pain and the body, you'll find there are so many variables that contribute to the rise of illness and disease within us. It is not black and white or about ticking off a checklist of symptoms to arrive at a diagnosis.

Our body is incredibly sophisticated and, therefore, complex when it comes to masking an imbalance that has developed.

My personal research into chronic pain has been like opening a Pandora's box of all the unlimited causes that can contribute to one's imbalances. It's often about digging deeper than you first thought, sifting through, and discovering the connection between your mind and body. You sift through the layers and then piece together what's relevant to your situation and pain and what's not but may apply for someone else. Every case of chronic pain is unique to the individual and what they've been through.

Even with my personal interest and lengthy investment in understanding chronic pain, finding reputable sources and information about it has been incredibly challenging. I'm happy to report that finally, slowly, science is starting to delve into how the body responds to signals from the mind, particularly around how emotions are processed and stored within the body, how they can manifest and present as pain, how this can further perpetuate physical imbalance and disease, how the mind can exacerbate this imbalance and produce further physical consequences, and how this pile-up of issues can continually impact one's mental, emotional, and physical experiences within the body. Once you start to look closely, the situation becomes complicated.

However, we're still in the early stages of a healthcare revolution. We're only now starting to realise that we can't simply manage pervasive conditions by suppressing their symptoms. This approach doesn't work for many individuals, as the pain often continues, increases, or fades temporarily only to return. Society, medicine, and governments are slowly opening up to the broader causes contributing to our pain epidemic.

Soon, we'll delve into how we can start to expand our view of chronic pain, but in order to do that, we must first understand why we think the way we do.

DEFINING INVISIBLE AND CHRONIC ILLNESSES

Defining and diagnosing invisible illness and chronic pain is challenging, no matter one's medical background or teachings. Anything that can't be seen with the physical eye or doesn't appear in diagnostic testing is understandably difficult for practitioners to recognise, let alone diagnose.

There are many conditions that fall under this category. Common invisible conditions include:

- Mental, genetic, and neurological conditions
- Chronic fatigue syndrome
- Chronic pain
- Fibromyalgia
- Autoimmune conditions
- Leaky gut
- Multiple sclerosis
- Post-concussive syndrome
- Endometriosis
- Infertility
- Depression and mental illnesses
- Allergies and food intolerances
- Digestive disorders such as celiac, colitis, and irritable bowel syndrome
- Lupus
- Lyme disease
- Post-traumatic stress disorder

As you can see, the list is broad.

It is proposed that up to a whopping 90 percent of people with disabilities live with an invisible illness or condition that has a physical chronic element and has either a mental or physical impairment on one's life and ability to perform everyday activities.[5] Chronic pain, chronic fatigue, and autoimmune conditions make up a group of conditions (which I fit into) that are often referred to as mystery illnesses. The ongoing discomfort and pain are often felt as muscular or joint pain or widespread, debilitating fatigue.

Many patients feel compelled (by themselves or doctors) to undertake extensive pathological testing, only to be told they appear to be perfectly fine.

> "A mystery illness is any ailment that leaves anyone perplexed for any reason ... so it's written off as a mental imbalance."
> –Anthony William[6]

In *The Disease Delusion*, written by Dr Jeffrey Bland, the founder of the functional medicine movement, he states that over the next 20 years, the cost of chronic disease on our global economy will be $47 trillion.[7] This is staggering when you consider how little we know about it or how we're going to address it from here.

One of the few published articles that explores the increase in chronic pain in Australia was published by the Australian Institute of Health and Welfare in 2020. It provided one of the first collections of data about the growing reality of chronic pain experienced by many Australians.

> The article reported:
> » 1 in 5 Australians aged 45 and over are living with persistent, ongoing pain.
> » In 2018, chronic pain cost Australia an estimated $139 billion and was associated with loss of quality of life and productivity.
> » Over the past ten years, patient encounters relating to chronic pain have increased by 67 percent for GPs.[8]

While it's acknowledged that chronic pain is subjective, doctors and practitioners are certainly *reporting* seeing more and more 'invisible illnesses' – conditions that are not considered chronic and don't necessarily show up on the standard tests, physically appear on the external body, or display empirically verifiable or measurable symptoms. However, they are impacting people's ability to function and perform everyday activities, and we must remember that is an important symptom in and of itself.[9]

The symptoms of invisible illness can vary from one person to another. We may experience pain, fatigue, other physical symptoms, mental health concerns, or all of the above. The long-held method of prescribing a pill, even when diagnosis isn't possible, is simply no longer feasible. **There is no one-size-fits-all approach when it comes to treating chronic illness and pain.**

> "Unfortunately the pill for an ill system is in no way suited to addressing the chronic illnesses that are today's health reality."
> –Dr Jeffrey S Bland[10]

While some research is underway, as long as there are so few answers and so little support available, we must look to ourselves and the knowledge our bodies contain to help those living with chronic pain.

While more research will help battle the rising cost of chronic illness and disease to the community, I'm also concerned about the increased cost (not just financial but mental, emotional, and physical) of chronic pain to the individual. Continually managing an invisible illness and getting validation and support in a world where alternative therapies are a massive out-of-pocket expense can create huge financial strain, especially for those who can't work due to illness-related limitations and where lack of funding is unavailable to such individuals.

THE QUEST FOR VALIDATION

Not being heard or believed, or not receiving an actual diagnosis, leaves patients feeling frustrated on so many levels. Many conditions can overlap with autoimmune conditions, making detection even harder. This lack of diagnosis can make patients feel dismissed by their doctors and often their loved ones. Even if we can agree that measuring chronic pain is exceedingly difficult because pain is such a subjective experience, *validating* someone's experience of chronic pain, even if it can't be conventionally measured, is important.

The unseen cost of not feeling validated can have significant ramifications, and individuals may feel constantly shamed, ignored, or even gaslit. The undermining of their experience causes a huge impact on their emotional and mental welfare. Acknowledgment and support are so crucial for the person experiencing pain so they can move forward with optimism and options. Lack of validation creates more stress and inaction, exacerbating the situation.

I hope to see professionals asking very targeted, discerning questions of their patients – questions about the possible causes of their chronic pain and linking the potential connections to stress and trauma. While I understand the time pressures placed upon 21st-century medical practitioners, taking the time to listen and ask questions of the patient is crucial. The lack of diagnosis, the lack of awareness, the lack of understanding, and the lack of empathy take a huge toll.

All of these challenges around the pressures of cost, validation, and support can further complicate the manifestation of pain. It becomes a cycle that's hard to identify and break out of. The 'burdens' that arise from seeking treatment and not succeeding can further affect our body's mentally, emotionally, and physically, in addition to everything else the patient has to endure on a day-to-day basis.

As you can see, discussion around invisible illnesses is multifaceted. Defining chronic pain, evaluating attitudes and stigmas, sourcing statistics, feeling validated, and finding the right treatment and support can be extremely complicated.

To help us begin breaking the rules of pain, I have summarised the current existing challenges that we need to address around chronic pain. Some of them are societal challenges, and some of them will be up to the individual. Regardless, they are challenges we must start to overcome.

TABLE OF CHALLENGES

1. Recognition: The first challenge is the concept of chronic pain and invisible illnesses being recognised within medical circles and accepted without judgement within broader society. Even though chronic pain as a condition only began to be considered officially by Western medicine in recent decades, debate about chronic pain without obvious pathological symptoms began to emerge over a century ago.[11] Chronic pain has been experienced for a very long time, yet there continue to be numerous stigmas around chronic pain and invisible illnesses and their validity as a medical condition.

2. Limited approach: The Western medicine model primarily treats pain by reducing acute symptoms. Rarely does it delve further to assess how one's external environment and internal workings contribute to one's experience of inflammation, which in turn creates pain. More holistic modalities need to be considered for each individual.

3. Mind-Body connection: There is limited understanding and acceptance of the relationship between psychology and physiology, including mind-body disorders. This could be due to the rise of scientific inquiry in the past few centuries as well as conditioning from previous generations.

4. Limited funding: There is limited funding available to invest in research because chronic pain is so broad and 'invisible'. Funding and research seem to be directed towards the more known conditions.

5. Accurate information: Accurate information and statistics are hard to find because chronic pain and invisible illness are such subjective experiences, making it difficult to create a benchmark. Ascertaining the number of people actually living with invisible illnesses is further complicated if we look at studies that highlight that people living with hidden disabilities may wish to remain anonymous, as they "do not fit into either category of being disabled or able bodied."[12] Further, some clinicians may accuse patients with invisible illnesses of being dishonest, expressing frustration and dismissing any symptoms as psychosomatic.[13]

6. Interchangeable terminology: When practitioners diagnose patients with an invisible illness, they sometimes label it an illness and sometimes a disability. The terms are used interchangeably, which adds considerable confusion. We need to remember that any diagnosis and treatment will be subjective and based on the individual practitioner's training and personal viewpoint.

7. Attitudes to alternative medicines: Overcoming scepticism around alternative and holistic therapies is crucial. More people are, in fact, gravitating towards such treatments to help support them in living with chronic illness. Current limitations and frustrations with the way chronic pain is managed and treated has seen an increasing emergence of integrative medicine or integrative health (also known as complementary or alternative health and medicine).

Numerous individuals have told me firsthand that they first ventured down this 'alternative' path when their doctor wasn't able to provide them with a diagnosis and they felt lost within a system that couldn't support them.

In one study that examines integrative medicine in Australia and New Zealand, the authors conclude that both countries could benefit from an "integrative medicine practice-based research network" to conduct relevant research and inform policy.[14]

There is a growing integration between Western and alternative medicine, leading to the consideration of multiple factors that could be contributing to certain conditions and pain. However, there needs to be more of an integration between traditional medicine and holistic therapies in the management

> and support of patients. We should aim to better guide patients to adjust their lives if they do receive a diagnosis and teach them to manage or treat the pain while getting on with their lives. They don't need to let the pain take over.

A VERY PERSONAL CASE STUDY

Let's turn all that we've been discussing towards focusing on real-life scenarios that show the nuances and unique circumstances that must be considered case by case when helping someone unravel their chronic pain. For this, I'll use my own journey and case notes.

> **Name**: *Amie Rule*
> **Sex**: *Female*
> **Age**: *40s*
> **Occupation**: *Energy and Chronic pain Coach*
> **Symptoms**: *Chronic fatigue, major pelvic and back pain*
> **First appeared**: *Early 20s, incapacitating back pain while working in a jewellery store, many weeks off work to recover, occurred numerous times.*
> **Major health challenge/s**: *Extreme pelvic pain during pregnancies, many days unable to walk.*
> **Other factors at play**: *High-pressure job in her 20s and 30s, past childhood and teen trauma.*

Medical evaluation: *After seeing numerous specialists, having numerous tests that were inconclusive or couldn't determine the origin of pain, was eventually diagnosed with fibromyalgia at the age of 36.*
Alternative Treatments: *Physiotherapy, kinesiology, chiropractic care and support, neurofeedback, neuroprogramming, quantum healing, Chinese medicine, naturopathy, remedial massage, Bowen therapy.*

My own case notes provide an example of illness being present but not seen, and there's a lot more to the story. From the time of my first back episode, over the years I've had countless tests and scans, which have shown very little in terms of Western symptoms.

When assessing my bloods, it highlights that I have a below-average white cell count. Our white blood cells are crucial for fighting off infection, and their absence can be an indication of neutropoenia. Over the last 15 years, my white cell count has ranged from close to 1.0 to 3.2. An average person ranges from 4 to 12. My levels, despite being low, are fine, as I still have the ability to fight off infection.

My bloods do show that I present with some autoimmune markers, which indicates that I am susceptible to autoimmune conditions. However, most doctors will read this as me having *no* autoimmune markers.

I do, however, have a history of low iron, irritable bowel syndrome, nutritional deficiencies, osteopenia, and endometriosis. The rest of my bloods also appear within the normal range;

however, the normal range can be quite expansive, and sitting on the lower range of normal can indicate other issues.

It's only when you start to delve into the wider range of testing, such as hair and skin analysis, gut microbiome and stool testing, that you can start to get a clearer picture of what is occurring within your body and how all of this produces the particular symptoms you're experiencing.

When doctors solely rely on bloods to make a diagnosis, the truth is often missed.

WHY IS THERE SUCH LIMITED UNDERSTANDING?

The overarching question (which gave rise to this book) that we need to ask ourselves, as individuals and as a society is: Why aren't we looking at all possible variables and factors that could be causing such a rise in invisible conditions? Are we so conditioned to symptoms-based medicine and attitudes that we can't see the older and innate knowledge that lies beyond those boundaries?

In her successful book, *Why People Don't Heal and How They Can*, Caroline Myss explains that sometimes illness is the result of a complexity of causes and it's futile to try to fix the cause based on a single, simple factor.[15] In my opinion, this is what the traditional Western science and medical model tries to do. Myss elaborates that sometimes illness develops due to our increasingly toxic environment, as well as exposure to germs, bacteria, and viruses. Illnesses can also be attributed to contaminated water and parasites; others can be due to a genetic predisposition.[16]

For a smart species, human beings can be surprisingly slow to learn and quick to forget. In the past, we turned to home remedies, such as ginger for nausea, chicken soup for colds, and aloe vera for burns, to help our bodies heal. Nowadays, however, these simple yet effective solutions are often overlooked.

Complementary therapies, such as acupuncture, herbal medicine, and meditation, do have a place alongside conventional medicine, and we're beginning to relearn what we've forgotten. Slowly, a wider variety of integrative attitudes are emerging in the Western model. A report published in 2021 highlighted that, in Australia, at least 30 percent of GPs have reported practising integrative medicine and prescribing and recommending integrative therapies. These therapies can include nutrition-based supplements (as opposed to prescription-based) and mind-body practices, such as yoga, meditation, and acupuncture. It's important to note that, in this report, integrative medicine refers to "therapies and medicines that are not conventionally used by medical doctors, but which may complement medical management and, thus, be successfully integrated into medical practice."[17]

This type of approach isn't just symptoms-based but focuses on the patient's mind, body, and spirit as part of the healing process.[18] The emergence of allied health workers to support, treat, and diagnose individuals is growing. While literature states that there's no official term to describe these workers, they generally sit outside of medical, dental, and nursing professions. Nevertheless, these practitioners are specialised experts within their fields and can assist to diagnose, treat, and prevent a range of conditions.

Allied health is generally multidisciplinary and works in conjunction with medical professionals to treat and care for patients. Interestingly, allied health practitioners and integrative practitioners do use evidence-based research and training to determine how to assist individuals to "protect, restore and maintain optimal physical, sensory, psychological, cognitive, social and cultural function."[19]

Because you're reading this book, I encourage you to look for these progressive types of practitioners who are open to recommending integrative therapies (in addition to Western therapies). We don't need to choose one over the other. We can leverage them collectively, and even if you face resistance in the form of not being heard and not being presented with all the options, please know there are alternatives! There are people out there who will hear you, guide you, and support you in the capacity you need.

The crux of it is that you need to open the door to receiving help and guidance, which can mean asking for help in a new way that you're yet to explore. Educate yourself, be open to new experiences, and keep growing to support what your body requires in order to heal itself.

MODERN PRESSURES THAT CONTRIBUTE TO THE CHRONIC PAIN PANDEMIC

The manual demands of our lives may well have decreased over the last few centuries; however, other challenges have arisen in their place. Managing the significant mental, emotional, and psychological demands in modern times is something our ancestors could never have imagined or foreseen.

Similarly, there is a growing awareness of the effects of the manufactured environments we now live in. For much of our lives, many of us are surrounded by concrete jungles and exposed to harmful plastics, toxic fumes, electromagnetic fields, and incessant stress. The factors behind the growing statistics on chronic or undiagnosed pain have emerged over a number of centuries and have become multifaceted. I summarise them as four main pressures or categories.

> ### FAST LIFE, FAST FOOD
> We no longer prioritise our health and wellbeing; instead, we prioritise our work and generating an income. We've been taught and raised to believe that our end goal in life is to work, move up the corporate ladder, and keep working until we retire. In this modern world, not only are we working longer hours, but we're also a lot more sedentary, opting to sit at desks in front of computers for prolonged periods. We're indoors for

the majority of the day, resulting in a lack of exposure to vitamin D derived from sunshine. We've become so busy with life and keeping up with the status quo that we rely heavily on fast foods, convenience foods, food laden with preservatives, additives, and colours, processed foods that are quick and easy to make but are just temporary fillers.

You only need to go into a supermarket to see countless shelves lined with packaged, tinned, and processed foods. Most supermarkets have only one aisle dedicated to healthy foods, foods that are actually considered far from the 'norm' of the processed and packaged foods we've grown accustomed to. Our reliance on fast food means that we have become disconnected from how natural foods are grown, and, in turn, we disregard the importance of freshly grown produce as a central part of a healthy diet, resulting in diets that aren't nutrient-dense. Our obsession with ease has created an increase in disease.

ISOLATED LIVING

We're becoming more isolated and more disconnected from people and even ourselves. Technology and work demands mean less time for connection to others, connection to community, connection to nature, and even connection to ourselves. Instead, these have been replaced with an increased pace of life, increased stress, increased connection to and reliance on technology, creating a more sedentary lifestyle. We rely on technology to replace the gaps of boredom and to replace heartfelt connection.

In addition to this, we're so out of tune with doing the things that make us and our bodies feel good, and many of us are used to feeling isolated, alone, lacklustre, sluggish, tired, and fatigued. This has become our norm in our fast-paced world. As much as technological advancements have advanced our capabilities, living in a data-centric world means we've forgotten crucial elements of life, like the importance of nature, movement, community, and togetherness.

Long gone are the traditional, primal ways of living in a close-knit village. In the primal era, when women and men lived in small communities, away from commercialisation, they were honoured and respected for their roles within the community and family unit. Today, we're so used to living in solitude, so independent from one another that we've lost the ability to connect with others. We've also forgotten the importance of community in raising kids. Modern living has caused us to isolate ourselves and become deaf to our body's primal signals and messages.

GERM PHOBIA

We live in an overly clean and sterile world, which has resulted in compromised immune systems. In *The Nourishing Traditions Book of Baby & Childcare* – a somewhat controversial book because it focuses on the traditional, ancient ways of raising children, similar to our parents' and grandparents' – the authors highlight that the sterile environments in which we are living and raising our children are negatively impacting our body's ecosystems, denying us many of the bacteria we need for a healthy, balanced microbiome.[20]

Our gut microbiome plays a huge role in regulating how our body functions. It helps us control our weight and fight off infection. It also influences inflammation, regulates our sleep, impacts our mood, and so much more. So, when our gut microbiome is compromised (due to one or more of the mentioned factors), so is our overall health.

Over the years, we've seen a global increase in the frequency of antibiotic prescriptions by medical professionals, often prescribing even when the infection is viral rather than bacterial.[21] While immunisation and antibiotic treatment have reduced the spread of infectious disease, the increased use of medication in the general population adds another complexity when analysing the increase in chronic illness and disease and evaluating the inadvertent impact prescription drugs might have on existing conditions.[22] Antimicrobial resistance has increased so much that it's now considered a global public health challenge. There's an enormous gap in knowledge and research around the consequences of overprescribing medication and its potential contribution to the development and onset of chronic illness.

OVER-STIMULATION

We're exposed to so much more stimuli than ever before in human history. From the moment we wake to the seconds before we close our eyes, we're constantly being stimulated. We're bombarded with masses of information day in and day out as we work ever longer hours. There are more requirements for us now as parents and as working individuals. We're constantly on the go, with little downtime. Our fast-paced lifestyles are becoming the norm, but they're also creating a burden on our nervous system because we so rarely switch off.

Our current pace of life means that many of us are overworked and stressed out, ignorant of the impact this stress is causing on our nervous system and our overall body. Not only are we dealing with massive amounts of information, but we're also exposed to an influx of chemicals, toxins, and pressures from all avenues, placing a heavy burden on our body as it tries to gather, process, and store information. **This modern way of living is not only causing physical fatigue but also neurological fatigue.**

Contrary to our old way of thinking, stress is no longer simply nervous tension but is rather considered "a measurable set of objective physiological events in the body, involving the brain, the hormonal apparatus, the immune system and many other organs."[23] When looking at the causes of stress to the body, we need to delve deeper to understand all the areas in our life that are creating physiological disharmony and potentially presenting symptoms of pain. Even more interesting,

> we're realising that stress can occur without the expression of nervous tension.[24]

YOUR PAIN IS A MESSAGE

Now it's time to break down our preconceived notions of pain — what we know, or think we know, about pain in general. From a biological perspective, our body communicates to us in many unseen ways, signalling to our brain when we're too hot or too cold, hungry or thirsty, experiencing high and low blood sugar levels, and so on.

They're all uncomfortable feelings that tell us our body isn't in balance. Our internal homeostasis needs attention; otherwise, our body's health and function will deteriorate, sometimes seriously! That's why we spend much of the day fulfilling our body's needs: eating and drinking and maintaining an optimal temperature, no matter what environment we're in. These unconscious messages ensure our survival and wellbeing.

> By the same token, pain is also a message, signal, or communicator, telling us that some part of our body is not operating as it was designed to.

For example, it could be sudden, acute pain, which is generally the result of direct tissue, muscular, or bone injury – the most common type of pain we experience. Your first memory of pain is likely related to a typical childhood mishap, perhaps when you fell off your bike or out of a tree. You no doubt scraped and injured yourself, possibly even broke an arm or a leg, and you can probably still recall the pain of impact, even after all these years.

From an early age, we learn that engaging in certain activities involves risk of injury and, therefore, physical pain. An acute pain response doesn't need to be significant. It can involve something as minor as cutting your finger, burning your hand on a hot stove, or stubbing your toe. When this happens, our nerve endings use pain to signal to our brain that there is an injury. Our brain can then signal to the rest of the body to pump blood urgently to that area. Because of this, many direct physical injuries are easy to diagnose and treat, as we can identify the cause and the impact on the body.

Due to their early experience with pain, most children quickly develop an awareness of how to avoid it. Evolution has helped us associate a pain response with being negative, which helps us better evaluate our environment for risks and, therefore, limit our injuries. Considering the concept of pain from a survival perspective, it's understandable how our responses cause us to believe that all pain is bad and stems from a direct cause that we must try to avoid. Thus, we have created a negative association with pain. When we experience chronic or invisible pain, with no diagnosis or validation, the negative emotions increase towards the pain, becoming anger and resentment towards our body as a whole.

When breaking the rules of pain, we must take a more proactive yet gentle approach while looking at our pain objectively. Exploring and understanding the broad areas of 'functional' pain will show you the layers of pain and imbalances (without obvious cause) that become issues that mount upon each other in a confusing mass of chronic pain. Our body's processes are so intricately connected and reliant on all parts working as they were designed that even when a tiny part isn't functioning optimally, it can affect the whole system. Exploring what's happening internally will help us create a wider understanding of why pain is present and why it has originated.

THE PROMINENT ROLE OF INFLAMMATION

Pain and inflammation go hand in hand. If you have an injury, it's likely that you will be recommended both pain relief and an anti-inflammatory to treat both the pain and the inflammation. We can think of the occurrence of inflammation as the body's defence against infections, injuries, toxins, and anything else detrimental.[25]

In actual fact, an inflammatory response can occur within any part of our body. Inflammation is actually a natural response that occurs when the immune system is doing its job by attempting to stop further injury and prompt recovery.[26] If the cause of injury is evident – for example, a fall, a cut, a broken bone – it is easier to ascertain how the body reacts because we can see or detect what's occurring within the body.

Chronic inflammation can have a negative impact on one's organs and tissues and can lead to a number of different health conditions that fall within the autoimmune category. It can lead to the immune system attacking healthy cells, mistaking them for foreign invaders.[27] However, because we can't see what's occurring within our body, we don't know how much inflammation is actually present.

My experiences have shown that practitioners often give insufficient attention to the link between the cause of inflammation and the presence of chronic physical pain. Physicians are trained to primarily look at how to reduce the acute symptoms and will prescribe medication to reduce the inflammation and the pain signals. Rarely will they look at the different variables behind the excessive inflammation in the first place or delve into the 'why' and 'what' of your history that might reveal the cause behind it.

The assessment of causal factors seems to be missing within the medical industry, where it all falls into the too-hard basket. When pain becomes prolonged and creates chronic inflammation, further imbalance and (invisible) disease will develop, so the journey can become quite complicated for physicians and for you as the patient.

> If we're not addressing what's causing the increased inflammation, we can't remove the cause of the pain.

For the last two decades, I have researched and studied extensively to understand the nature of fibromyalgia, chronic pain, and autoimmune disorders. Notwithstanding the complexity and subjectivity of my particular circumstances, I believe that excessive toxic load and excessive trauma impacted my body in such a way that it caused a huge inflammatory response. This, in turn, compromised my immune system, which went on to affect my nervous system so significantly it created the onset of fibromyalgia.

From working with clients and from personal experience, chronic inflammation is a slow burn. The 'normal' inflammatory response becomes prolonged, and pain persists for months and even years. This, in turn, starts to create problems within all the other areas of the body, and instead of inflammation remaining localised, it starts to spread throughout the whole body.

In his book, *The Disease Delusion*, Jeffrey Bland looks to dispel some of the myths surrounding chronic illness. Bland writes that we are now seeing the emergence of diseases that are becoming chronic – that is, "all those conditions, ailments and illnesses that make you sick and then never really go away."[28] I am strongly inclined to think the emergence and greater incidence of disease is because of the huge pressures, stress, trauma, lack of awareness around our bodies, and the inability to discern the early warning signs of illness. Too many times, we leave it too late.

> Unfortunately, our modern lifestyles are contributing to different types of chronic pain that we're not accustomed to – prolonged pain that we don't have a broad, open-minded understanding of. I believe that teaching people a holistic, integrated approach to discovering and treating the source of inflammation, disease, and pain can significantly reduce the incidence and impact of chronic pain for many people.

Let's look at some other examples. As a little girl, I was riddled with eczema and dry skin. This was a by-product of my orphanage environment. There were only short periods of time scheduled for outside play, and my exposure to direct sunlight was very limited. This meant my body produced far less than the recommended amount of vitamin D for growing bodies. Lack of vitamin D causes rickets, which results in softened bones and reduced bone density.

Lack of proper nutrition also created an inflammatory response all over my skin (the skin being our largest organ), and it showed up as eczema. Many of us simply relate eczema to dry, irritated skin. When we go to a doctor, they treat it topically with a steroid-based cream, which is fine to address the surface issue temporarily. But if you look at it at a deeper level, eczema is most often linked to gut health.[29] If you address the gut issues or the gut imbalances you have, the problem will resolve itself over time and reduce the likelihood of future occurrences.

Eczema and psoriasis can also be linked to too much heat and too much 'fire' within the body, which is linked to inflammation. Therefore, it takes a multipronged approach to identify the cause, support and heal the gut, and reduce the heat (inflammation) within the body to consequentially heal the external skin. However, for many, this is either too costly or requires too much time. As a society, we've been conditioned to expect a quick return and if this doesn't happen, it's an inconvenience in our busy lives.

Imbalances within us are often represented in our skin condition. Acne is another example of a hormonal imbalance within the body and can occur for many reasons. Yet again, often we'll go to a doctor who will prescribe Roaccutane but fail to look at the different influences, including diet and environmental factors, that could be causing the acne.

Similarly, my husband Rhys experienced a few health conditions to do with skin and allergy issues. Nothing to be alarmed about, but with a family history of diabetes and autoimmune disorders, I knew that this would keep having an impact on him. Yet despite him experiencing a lifetime of psoriasis and gut issues, not one doctor felt the need to speak to him about the relevant considerations when it came to managing his health. In actual fact, after performing the basic blood and heart tests, his doctor reported him to be 'perfect'. This is one of the issues with blood tests. If the results sit within the norm or the average, you're considered healthy, even 'perfect', even if your ongoing issues indicate otherwise.

I lovingly told Rhys that his body was telling him it was feeling far from 'perfect'. His body, skin, allergies, and fatigue highlighted that there was something more pressing underneath all the layers. This proves again how hard it is to determine what's occurring within us. Many males consider this a natural occurrence, accepting that fatigue comes with age. Our medical industry also isn't designed to look at preventative measures to assist individuals with their health, and often it's only when we encounter a full-blown health condition and our body experiences so much pain, with alarm bells ringing loudly, that we finally pay attention.

Our lack of awareness is due to our lack of education. Many of us have systemic chronic inflammation occurring within our bodies without realising what it is. For Rhys, we're now undertaking further testing with a kinesiologist, including hair and mineral testing, which will allow us to understand the underlying issues within his body.

Many of my clients who experience chronic health conditions feel like they've been on a constant merry-go-round, searching for answers yet being told they're perfectly fine when they don't feel fine. They feel defeated by the system, the lack of education, and the lack of choice available to them.

THE TRUE MEANING OF DISEASE

Many of us were fortunate in our younger years to have functioned in a state of effortless ease. We could run and jump and climb as we instinctively tested our young body's capabilities. Movement and motion were so easy we didn't even think about what we were doing. If we reflect on the origin of the word 'disease', it is made up of the Latin prefix 'dis', meaning 'away', and the suffix 'ease', translating to 'away from ease'. So 'disease' was anything that moved us away from this state of 'ease', and initially it was used in written terms to describe moments of trouble, discomfort, or distress many centuries ago. In modern use, it has evolved to mean being sick or ill, or to have some sort of bodily dysfunction.[30] The heart of its meaning remains the same though, referring to a lack of ease or harmony within the body, and this imbalance results in the onset of an illness or disease. Our body wants to recover that state of 'ease', just like when we were younger.

Most modern Western upbringings enforce the idea that in order to reduce symptoms and remove pain, we need to go to a pharmacist or doctor to buy pain relief medication or external treatments. For example, when you have a headache, you take paracetamol. If you have a sports injury, you're instructed to take an anti-inflammatory to reduce inflammation. Many women from my era would have a firm recollection of experiencing period pain and being told to take Naprogesic, fill up a hot water bottle, and get some bed rest. Yet many of these conditions, which are complex and multifaceted, hard to diagnose, and don't benefit simply from a quick fix or even a long-term fix, are confusing to many practitioners and specialists. However, to the individual's experiencing them, they are painful and chronic.

Despite its serious effects, it's astonishing how little awareness there is around how to manage and treat chronic pain. But there are understandable reasons when we consider, for example, that fibromyalgia can appear as muscular and joint pain as well as fatigue, among a number of other symptoms. This wide array of symptoms confuses practitioners, who will treat the muscular pain and tension but don't have the understanding (or time) to delve into the underlying factors that are causing the pain.

It's slowly becoming more understood that complex conditions, such as fibromyalgia and autoimmune conditions, don't magically appear overnight. They've been a long time coming and are generally a product of many factors, including genetics, modern-day nutritional deficiencies, stress, trauma, and lifestyle factors, which have created pressure on one's immune system, creating issues in the nervous system, which in turn creates additional problems in the whole body. So many variables can impact the dysfunction of the body, creating an imbalance. Learning about how these variables are related and can compound is imperative to breaking the rules of pain.

LISTEN TO THE TELLTALE SIGNS

The crucial fact is that no one tells us that pain is there as a communication tool to bring our attention to the imbalance within the body. Crippling period pain isn't supposed to be normal; neither are stomach pains or continual back pain. These are all our body's way of communicating that something is wrong. When we ignore these signals, they continue to get worse.

The thought of examining our internal workings can be daunting. For many people, it's easier to simply ignore the messages and try to suppress the pain rather than ask questions and give their body and rest and nurturing it needs.

As I've shown, society is seeing the emergence (and increase) of invisible illnesses such as chronic fatigue syndrome and autoimmune conditions like rheumatoid arthritis and fibromyalgia, where the body experiences physically debilitating chronic pain but without a visible cause or known medical reason. However – through no fault of our own – often, we don't understand all the different factors that could explain what caused the imbalance in the first place. Far more challenging to understand are the internal imbalances that aren't a result of direct physical injury.

So, when we can't eliminate this type of pain (or when it becomes prolonged), we wonder why our body can't heal despite all the 'treatments' we're being given. We wonder what's 'wrong' with us. We wonder why nothing external is working.

But I'm here to tell you that nothing is wrong with you; you don't need fixing.

> Unaccountable pain is often from an accumulation of stress, trauma, experiences, and psychological pressure that results in internal physical reactions. The body compensates for what the mind hasn't processed and released yet, and this imbalance can cause a prolonged physical, painful response within the body.

REDEFINING CHRONIC PAIN

This is your first step in breaking the rules of pain: redefining how you think about chronic pain. It's time to create a new mindset.

> To create this new mindset, you need to acknowledge the following statements:
> - We have never been taught that pain can be a product of the accumulation of stress and trauma within our body.
> - We have never been taught that the build-up of stress manifests in numerous internal and external conditions that deviate from our body's natural function.

> » We have never been taught that pain can mean a physical, emotional, or chemical imbalance within the body.
> » We have never been taught how to delve deeply past the superficial aspects of our pain.
> » When we can't suppress or mask the pain, we wonder why we have failed.
> » We have never been taught that experiencing symptoms of pain does not mean that we are broken and faulty.

Now, think about your current perspective of pain, the underlying narrative and where it came from. Are your beliefs regarding pain obtained from your parents, from your peers, from your practitioners or specialist, or a combination of all the above? What thoughts and beliefs do you carry around your own symptoms and experiences? Have you accepted the belief that you're broken and at fault?

OUR NERVOUS SYSTEM IS EXHAUSTED

Beyond the complexities of finding treatment for individuals, we must consider the long-term impact chronic pain and stress have on the body. We know that when stress occurs, there's a discharge from our nervous system to alert our brain of an immediate danger. Our body, in turn, undertakes numerous changes (including hormonal and immune) to survive these perceived threats.[31] But the important question is: What happens to the body when this stress, this threat is long-term, chronic, and continues being felt for months or even years? What are the consequences of continual pain and stress on the body over such a long period of time?

Biologically, a fight-or-flight response is triggered in extreme situations, which originally applied to an impending animal attack. People literally had to run or fight for their lives.

Nowadays, this threat is rarely a physical danger (you'd be unlucky to have to escape from a wild animal!), and the threats now come in the form of the many modern stresses I've explained, which means there are more of them more often. It's everyday circumstances that are causing individuals to feel stress or a perceived threat. However, many people are oblivious to the influx of stressors all around us. Compared to the past, we live under constant stress and constant stimulation. We live in denser, more populated cities, with greater mental and visual stimulation, greater exposure to wi-fi, electromagnetic fields, pollution, chemicals in the food we consume, as well as toxic chemicals within our household 'cleaning' products, which all cause – you guessed it – greater inflammation within the body!

We're also dealing with greater work demands, greater parenting demands, and greater pressures from a society that's moving at such a fast pace in every aspect. Stress is no longer just an external response but can also be triggered by a physical, biological, chemical, or psychological attack.[32] Therefore, it's understandable that many people are simply unaware of the impact that our everyday lives have on our body, let alone the perpetual cycle of fight and flight that negatively affects us.

This new definition of stress is one of the biggest factors in understanding the complexities of autoimmune conditions, pain conditions, and chronic fatigue. We're now seeing how things like our subjective experience of life, which includes emotions, trauma, and lifestyle, can cause stress within the body. This, in turn, impacts numerous bodily systems, weakening them and subsequently causing more stress and inflammation, which then leads to chronic pain.

For those with long-term chronic pain, a stress response is triggered a lot more easily than the 'average' person because of our already heightened nervous systems. A stress response is more easily triggered by simple things like the foods we consume, toxins we're exposed to, noises and bright lights, too much stimulation, lack of sleep, and stressful times. The perceived stress accumulates, and our body reactivates our parasympathetic nervous system to create another fight-or-flight response, which further impacts our nervous system, causing hormones to increase and our heart to race – all these wonderful things.

When this occurs day after day, week after week, and month after month, it becomes chronic. Even more to this, we're also realising that our brain can create the same stress response if we're exposed to the reactivation of a stressful memory. Even simply just the perceived threat of something stressful can cause such a response within our body.[33]

This adds even more to the complexity of the human body and understanding the causes of stress and trauma, and how the mind interprets them and any other continual perceived threats. We now understand that pain isn't just physical – it also has a mental component.[34] Understanding how both the brain and the mind play a part in this process is extremely important to shift the belief that pain is purely a physical experience or manifestation within the body.

WHY DOES THE BODY ATTACK ITSELF?

Acute pain causes a natural inflammatory response, but when the pain becomes chronic, it further stresses the body and impacts neural pathways to create a complex condition like fibromyalgia. The most important element to this, which not many doctors and practitioners are aware of, is the impact early exposure to stress and trauma has on our neurology and nervous system and how this flows on to every aspect of our body. When this cycle continues, it can create an autoimmune response.

Failing to treat this and suppressing the problems only contributes further to physical and mental symptoms and stress. As I described under the summary of modern pressures that contribute to our chronic pain pandemic, many of us are exposed to so many stressors that our grandparents were not: the amount of stimuli we are exposed to, the technological advancements that demand us to always be 'on' and instantly respond to text messages and emails, our work and personal commitments, and the city and urban practice of living on top of one another while, at the same time, being disconnected from one another. The infrastructure that comes with development has contributed to the increase in pollution, including toxic pollution, chemical exposure, and electromagnetic fields. How we manufacture food has also changed significantly, from depleted farming soil due to overuse, how animals are raised and pastured, all the way to how grains are produced genetically.

The commercialisation of the food industry means that our food has fewer nutrients, and more of it is being filled with additives and fillers. There's also a considerable increase in many fast-food options to meet the demands of our fast-paced lifestyle. When you combine all of this, plus work demands and home demands, many of us rarely see the light of day, which means we don't receive the benefits of nature or feel the sun on our body.

Our grandparents wouldn't have been exposed to the same level of neurotoxins that we're exposed to, either. Neurotoxins are toxins that are destructive to nerve tissue (causing neurotoxicity). Neurotoxicity refers to "damage to the brain or peripheral nervous system" caused by exposure to neurotoxins. Neurotoxins can "alter the activity of the nervous system" and the way our brains receive and process information.[35]

Neurotoxins can be found in common food products, cosmetic products, household products, pharmaceutical items, supplements, and even within the environment. They've become so prevalent that some academics are calling for further research to understand the impact of neurotoxin exposure on human neurocognitive ability.[36]

Another study highlights that there has been a significant increase in developmental neurotoxicity, but the issue resides in the fact that there's such limited data for most chemicals, including "environmental pollutants, industrial chemicals, drugs, consumer products, and food additives."[37] Research further posits that today one in six children is diagnosed with a developmental disorder, with environmental factors being a possible cause.

My personal experiences and the preceding information show how complex the body is when treating chronic pain and certain health conditions.

PRESCRIPTIONS AND PILLS DO NOT ALWAYS HEAL

As we've established, pain is a subjective experience that's extremely hard to quantify on a measurable scale. However, the first port of call we've been conditioned to go to is a general practitioner (GP). Unfortunately, this often means reaching for prescription drugs to mask the symptom and, therefore, mask the underlying cause as well.

There's an expectation in society that in order to fix pain, you need pills. That's how the majority of people in Australia have been raised, to believe solely in external guidance for help and healing.

> We rely on medication and quick fixes to do what the body is naturally capable of doing, given time.

At times, there may be a need to rely on medications to support the body in the healing process, but most of us are inclined to reach for the medicine cupboard to expedite the healing process. This becomes our default setting, and we've become so reliant on the conventional approach to heal our body that, over time, we've lost the conscious knowledge and awareness to naturally heal ourselves. This doesn't mean healing without assistance, guidance, and intervention. It means leveraging the deeper wisdom of all those around us, drawing upon it to determine what may be suitable for our body based on our experiences and allowing the body to heal on its own timeframe and trajectory.

While I say this, I know it can be hard to look outside the beliefs of our own operating systems. Yet that's exactly what Alberto Villoldo, researcher and medical anthropologist, was forced to do when, on a trip to South America, he picked up a variety of different parasites that lodged in his brain and caused his body to start shutting down. Villoldo, who also has a PhD in psychology and is a bestselling author, reflects that he should have died, but, as he approached a life-or-death situation, he felt compelled to leverage every tool known to man, from both Western medicine and ancient modalities, to not only heal his body but save his life.

From this experience, he realised that the majority of us are in a life and death struggle with the toxic forces that modern life throws at us. Many of us are prescribed anti-anxiety and antidepressant medications, but the problem still persists. Villoldo posits that **it is our bodies that heal**, a statement that holds immense possibilities.[38] However, our hierarchical medical system means that going to the GP or fulfilling prescriptions is often the only option that the majority of people are aware of.

We place all our hope and faith in our medical professionals to diagnose, treat, and cure us, and when we don't receive a diagnosis or any explanation, our belief in our doctors is shattered. We feel disheartened, disillusioned, and disappointed.

In some instances, people are misdiagnosed or prescribed a pill that won't ever address the cause. Other times, when tests reveal nothing out of the ordinary, people (like me) often feel like a failure or fraud, being told that the pain could be psychosomatic and not real.

Generally, doctors are quick to diagnose and prescribe a pill to address the presenting symptoms. In most cases, this is easier and cheaper than looking at the lifetime of variables contributing to the imbalance.

Today, there seems to be a pill for every state we find ourselves in, from numbing the mind when it's too active to numbing the body from pain, none of which addresses the actual cause of the pain or provides ways for people to shift the stigmas attached to the pain. Trust me, I've tried a whole bunch of them, mainly to alter the brain patterns that were either firing the pain or the ones that were impacting my mood. For me personally, neither worked and made me feel even more numb and disconnected from myself. For others, the pills do work, and this isn't a message to tell you to stop taking the pills. The message is urging you to look a little deeper into what your medication may be masking and take the time to delve into and invest in what your body is asking of you. In this day and age, we appear to be so consumed with everything else bar our health and wellbeing, and this attitude continues to reinforce our reliance on a system that may not have our best interests at heart. We're giving our power away to the medical system to suppress the symptoms, yet wondering why we're not getting better. More often than not, healing comes from all the choices we make to better ourselves and our life, and this means stepping away from our reliance on others and rather looking inward and listening intently to ourselves.

It's a case of Stockholm syndrome – we're held hostage by a system we so desperately want to diagnose, validate, and fix us. We keep searching through a broken system to fix us, and when it can't, we believe we must be the one at fault, which can dramatically affect our mental health. Yet we continue to seek solace in the system that has contributed to our ill health, often hoping for a diagnosis, for some part of our condition at least. However, diagnosis can pose a challenge, too.

THE DUALITY OF A DIAGNOSIS (RELIEF OR LIMITATION?)

Some people see a diagnosis as the path to validation. Having our pain diagnosed and labelled by a qualified professional often gives assurance that it's not simply all in our head, we aren't imagining it, and we aren't hypochondriacs.

My personal experience highlights how conditioned we can become by a society that likes to work with clear labels and categories. I'll never forget the enormous sense of relief I felt when I was finally diagnosed with fibromyalgia. Back in 2016, there was still little information on the aetiology of the condition, so there was still very little help on how to heal my body – apart from taking pain meds, nerve blockers, and antidepressants.

Despite feeling a myriad of emotions, the most notable sense was feeling validated by a system that had previously not known how it could support me. From talking to others since then, I've learnt that this sense of relief from receiving a diagnosis can be monumental. A lovely client of mine in his 50s, who had also been diagnosed with fibromyalgia, told me that the day he received his diagnosis was the best day of his life. Understanding that there was a reason for his significant physical, mental, and emotional decline gave him a huge sense of relief. He went on to say that the second-best day of his life was meeting me and having the opportunity to share his experiences without being pitied but rather being heard. Other clients have also expressed relief in understanding and getting validation and an explanation for what is occurring internally. A diagnosis can be a wonderful thing. We finally have validation and a possible reason for why our body is performing or reacting a certain way.

However, a diagnosis can also become a self-fulfilling prophecy, predetermining our lives. Many of us take our diagnosis and let it predefine our lives based on the specialists' opinions and prognosis. Thereafter, we tell our subconscious and conscious minds that this is our way of life from now on. We accept it, and our body picks up on these thoughts and starts believing it must be so. A diagnosis can be a very heavy feeling when accepted without questioning further.

THE WEIGHT OF A WESTERN PROGNOSIS

For many of us with chronic pain, chronic fatigue, or autoimmune conditions, the road to diagnosis has been so long and arduous that the thought of managing the condition is overwhelming. Many practitioners fail to give individuals the skills and resources to understand the impact of their physical pain. They ignore the flow-on effect in other areas of their lives and how this may impact them emotionally and mentally. They neglect to help patients understand that they need to adjust their lives to adapt and to heal and to manage their pain.

> We also fail to normalise the loss and grief cycle attached to any traumatic event, including the diagnosis of a chronic health condition, and how this varies amongst individuals.

In Johann Hari's book, *Lost Connections*, he explores the causes of depression and examines the work of a clinical psychologist who has a specialty in bereavement. This psychologist noticed a pattern with patients in mourning and how psychiatrists managed this interaction. She identified a pattern where, soon after the death of a loved one, her patients were being diagnosed with clinical depression and prescribed antidepressants. She highlights that patients who were suddenly dealing with the complexities of life were being diagnosed with anxiety and depression, as opposed to understanding that the emotional response of grief causing depression is a natural by-product of an individual's life events and circumstances. Many of the individuals in the case study who were diagnosed with depression then started to question their own feelings and doubted themselves.[39]

When it comes to individuals receiving a chronic health diagnosis, we must be mindful to treat them with empathy and compassion, as opposed to using a blanket approach and pre-empting that they will become depressed. Although, if they do, we shouldn't guilt, shame, or blame them. Imagine being given a life sentence of chronic, pervasive pain that will worsen over time and may impact your cognitive ability and your ability to perform in everyday life. Would you expect to walk out the door with a smile? No, I wouldn't expect that either.

We need to consider the individual's environment, their experiences, and their emotional response and then normalise it while providing the strategies to express these responses in a healthy environment, as opposed to diagnosing them, causing the person to assume there's a mental imbalance (although sometimes there may be), and prescribing them an antidepressant. It's normal and part of life to allow someone to be in a natural state of sorrow and to encourage therapy, conventional or otherwise, should they require it.

CHRONIC PAIN AND ANXIETY

While it's good to remain objective to the circumstances that may cause depression, such as a significant loss, the statistics do suggest that chronic pain and mental health often go hand in hand (referred to as comorbidities or more than one diagnosis).

The link between depression and anxiety and chronic conditions, chronic pain, and invisible illness is complicated. How, and how closely, anxiety is linked to pain is unknown, as there are numerous factors that contribute to both conditions. We do know that, like pain, emotional and cognitive information also travels through the body's nervous system. Therefore, when people with pain conditions experience any level of anxiety, the anxiety "reinforces the pain signals" – a very hard cycle to break out of.[40]

When I was diagnosed with fibromyalgia, my rheumatologist prescribed me a bundle of drugs that included antidepressants, even though I had stated that I wasn't depressed; I was just struggling with the constant pain. There was no discussion around the fact that chronic pain can cause mental anguish or how the symptoms can impact mental health. There was no mention of different strategies to address this, and after a while, I realised that it was the lack of support structures to help me live a seemingly 'normal' life that was contributing to my anxiety. There was no encouragement to seek help from a counsellor or a psychologist. I was given drugs, full stop.

Recently, I saw a new specialist to try alternative therapies to treat my fibromyalgia. While he was much more open to the impact of trauma on the entire body and the need to heal that trauma, he still prescribed me antidepressants; the Western medical conventions run deep. Other clients have reported the same: their diagnoses have been bittersweet in the sense that there's finally an explanation for their pain, finally some sort of validation, but alongside this comes the prescription of numerous drugs to combat the physical pain. Yet they're still left with the emotional toll of living with an invisible illness and chronic pain.

It's a rare practitioner that says, "I understand your pain, and I can see that this may be challenging." Instead, we're prescribed painkillers, nerve blockers, and antidepressants to manage the current pain and any further mental or physical issues that may arise. It feels like our pain is just swept under the carpet. It's a rotating door, walking in, being prescribed with the go-to selection of pain meds, walking out the door, and then the issues remain masked until another flare-up occurs and the process begins again, not to mention the long-term impact of taking prescription medicines on both the brain, the gut, and the body as a whole.

Many who are struggling with pain aren't actually mentally ill. They're simply struggling with the ongoing pain, the lack of understanding within the community, the lack of resources available to them, and, even more extreme, the resulting post-traumatic stress.

UNDERSTANDING MENTAL HEALTH, MENTAL ILLNESS, AND GRIEF

Let's expand on this a little further and delve into what mental health is, how it's viewed in modern-day society, and how this view can heavily impact someone with chronic pain. Mental health is defined as a person's condition regarding their psychological and emotional wellbeing. The World Health Organization defines mental health as "a state of mental well-being that enables people to cope with the stresses of life, realize their abilities, learn well and work well, and contribute to their community."[41]

Mental illness, on the other hand, can be defined as "a clinically diagnosable disorder that significantly interferes with an individual's cognitive, emotional or social abilities."[42] One of the most pressing issues that many face around the topic of mental health is the stigma attached to it. When they hear mental health, they often think of those with a mental illness rather than the fact that mental health is a component of overall health.[43]

Generally speaking, it's the role of a psychologist or psychiatrist to clinically diagnose an individual with a mental health condition or a psychological disorder. These are based upon a diagnostic tool called the *Diagnostic and Statistical Manual* (DSM), which is practically the bible of all diagnostic tools.

Johann Hari (*Lost Connections*) speaks of his personal experiences of being diagnosed with depression and using antidepressants, which, over an extended period, left him realising that he was becoming more depressed. This paradox motivated him to explore his experiences in depth and investigate why depression and anxiety are at epidemic levels.

In one chapter, entitled 'The Grief Exception', he explores how depression, according to the DSM, shares the same symptoms as grief. For example, to be considered clinically depressed, you need to show at least five out of nine symptoms nearly every day.[44] These symptoms include depressed mood, diminished interest or loss of interest in almost all activities, sleep disturbances, fatigue or loss of energy, feelings of worthlessness, and diminished ability to think or concentrate.[45]

However, due to this discovery that the symptoms of clinical depression match those of grief, the DSM was altered with a bereavement exclusion. While this may be a consideration for psychologists, psychotherapists, and psychiatrists, I wonder if this consideration will ever be made by doctors and clinicians when they're interacting with individuals experiencing chronic pain and invisible illness.

When I reflect on my experiences with managing chronic pain, I distinctly recall feelings of hopelessness and worthlessness within myself and my body. The constant pain caused me to feel tired and fatigued, and I did feel somewhat depressed; however, I can adamantly tell you that I wasn't clinically depressed. There's a distinction between feeling flat, depressed, and sad about your current situation versus being clinically depressed. That may be one of the most significant disconnections in the system.

My experiences studying psychology naturally gave me prior knowledge and awareness of this system, but many others diagnosed with fibromyalgia and pain are automatically prescribed antidepressants due to the mere assumption that chronic pain and mental health go hand in hand. Many studies on the topic are limited in that they don't have a benchmark – that is, they have no real basis for understanding someone's pain threshold and their individual ability to deal with stress.

They also don't consider the immense stress our bodies are already exposed to, as we wake up feeling fatigued every day, yet we've learnt to mask it and get on with life. No study acknowledges how chronic pain can cause a loss of one's identity and the grief associated with that. While we generally perceive grief to be associated with the death of a loved one, rarely do those treating chronic pain look at the grief from the loss of independence within the body, the loss of a previous life without chronic pain, and the loss of possible freedom.

Very important to note is that fibromyalgia also mimics some symptoms of depression, yet this is rarely discussed. A 2023 study that delves into fibromyalgia highlights that the systemic symptoms of this condition include cognitive dysfunction, sleep disturbances, anxiety, fatigue, and depressive episodes, which are all symptoms of depression.[46]

Over the past few years of living with fibromyalgia, I've had to do my own research to understand how fibromyalgia, which includes central sensitivity syndrome, can cause many systemic issues and also how our current way of living contributes to them. For example, how much of the everyday stress of modern life causes us to experience the stated symptoms? Some available research is helping us understand that cognitive dysfunction can also appear as brain fog – a general fogginess within the brain that causes memory problems, lack of mental clarity, poor concentration, and the inability to focus.[47] There's also research around the fact that things like brain fog, depression, reduced cognitive function, and lack of motivation are a result of inflammation in the brain, which can negatively affect the health of neurons.[48]

In previous sections, we highlighted how inflammation occurs to protect the body from injury. In doing so, our body initiates an inflammatory response to immobilise and stop our immune system in its tracks to prevent further damage and to repair the damage that's already done.[49] Unlike our immune system, our brain's immune cells don't have the ability to switch off to fight the perceived threat. Therefore, brain inflammation can move through the brain tissue slowly, damaging tissue and impacting brain function.[50] This systemic, chronic inflammation, which creates an autoimmune response, not only impacts the whole body but also the brain. Brain fog is a prominent symptom in individuals with autoimmunity, yet, for some reason, it's another symptom that's rarely discussed or managed to minimise further deterioration.

Over the years, I've noticed a huge cognitive decline. My procedural memory has deteriorated; my ability to absorb information has lessened, and my ability to stay on and engaged has reduced significantly. This in itself is cause for concern, and some would even say it has led to an increase in panic, fear, and anxiety that I've had to process while implementing strategies to help me function. If anyone's mental ability and mental health were impacted, I assume they would experience a similar response. However, instead of anticipating that this may happen, it's rarely even mentioned, so people walk away thinking they're the problem or they're mentally losing it.

In many cases, chronic pain conditions come with mental health challenges that not only include the stigma of living with an 'invisible' illness but also the controlling nature that depression and anxiety can have in the chronic pain cycle. It can feel debilitating and impossible to break out of.

As people continue to look for answers that don't exist in a Western medical model, hopelessness can create enormous mental and emotional anguish, which often compounds further physical stress.

CHRONIC PAIN AND ITS EFFECT ON MENTAL HEALTH

Let's now do a deeper dive into exactly how chronic pain can affect our mental health.

1. Pain affects the neural pathways, impacting our emotional state, psychological state, mental health, and physical health.

While psychologists are very much used to treating trauma within the body, we need to start recognising that chronic pain, especially in the long term, can also create trauma within the body. It can alter neural pathways and how we respond to pain; it can create default mechanisms to deal with pain, and it can cause us to disconnect from ourselves totally. Certain modalities, such as psychotherapy, tend to focus on the somatic body and encourage people to use mind-body principles and techniques to help them connect back to their body.

2. Pain can cause us to become sedentary.

Chronic pain can cause people to become restricted and sedentary. This decrease in movement can cause further health issues and impact hormones and mood. Feelings of anxiety and depression can cause people to be less healthy in their diet and routine, which can lead to extreme fatigue. This fatigue constantly impacts the nervous system and the body's pain signals, which further fatigues individuals.

3. Pain can cause increased levels of hopelessness.

From this point, it's important to understand that the feelings that come from experiencing all these challenges are normal. Anxiety, depression, confusion, feeling hopeless about the future, feeling uncertain of what life has to offer, struggling to make sense of what's happening within our physical body when diagnosed and living with chronic pain are normal. Yes, they're normal. Trying to process it is a huge adjustment, and all these feelings and emotions, doubt and uncertainty are how our body tells us it's struggling with processing it all, in addition to struggling with the actual pain.

A 2020 news report indicated that Australia has around 300 pain management specialists for the approximately 3.37 million people experiencing chronic pain. The wait lists for these pain clinics range from 12 months to five years, and during this time, people are suffering more and more from not only their physical pain but also their emotional pain.[51]

It's often the physical and emotional pain that's most debilitating, as we're always trying to find resources and practitioners to help us live a life with chronic pain. **The lack of resources available to support individuals with chronic pain is contributing to the mental and emotional anguish within many people.**

4. The financial burden and out-of-pocket expenses to manage pain can be considerable, putting further pressure on individuals.

For someone with a persistent chronic condition, the ongoing costs of care and medication can be a financial burden. The situation can be further exacerbated when pain and disability interfere with our ability to work. Combine financial stress with everything else, and mental health can suffer.

We need to normalise the impact that chronic pain can have on our mental health and what this may look like. Pain Australia reports that major depression is the most common mental health condition associated with chronic pain, so there needs to be a shift in the stigmas around mental health, mental disorders, and mental illnesses.[52] We need to start having these conversations, enabling patients to become more connected with their bodies. We need medical practitioners to focus on a more integrated approach to treatment, where they support the individual to improve their mental health with practical measures, to create resilience, to not default and spiral down the path of further mental, physical, and emotional pain and anguish.

THE EFFECTS OF SHAME AND STIGMA

Lastly, I want to draw your attention to the fact that physical pain brings on a massive subset of emotional and mental anguish that we haven't touched on, but it needs to be addressed. We must understand how our mindset is created. The link between how we're treated and categorised by specialists and physicians can have a considerable impact on our mindset and our perception of ourselves, adding additional stress on top of the chronic pain or illness already present.

Intertwined in the relationship between chronic pain and mental health is another lesser-known emotional challenge that comes with chronic pain. Sometimes, it can be difficult to tell where the pain ends and the shame of it begins, the shame of a dysfunctional body and the limitations it puts on life.

For many years, we've been subliminally shaming people for having physical or mental issues. We need to understand that an individual's emotional state, the continued exposure to the stress along with the condition itself, exacerbates the issues even further until they don't know what to address first, the mental or physical challenges, and it all seems too much. At times, individuals may make choices to take prescription medication or supplements to relieve some of the burden that resides within them. It's not anyone else's right to judge us based upon this and to inflict shame upon any decision we make.

BUT WHAT'S WRONG WITH YOU?

After being diagnosed with cancer, Susan Sontag, an American writer and philosopher, explored the notion of illness as a metaphor. She delved into the stigmas attached to disease and the 'victim blaming' in the language people use to describe diseases.[53]

The Institute for Chronic Pain explains that the stigma around chronic pain is a significant and persistent problem for many. They define the stigma attached to chronic pain as "the criticism of being bad in some way for simply having a condition that you didn't choose to have."[54]

Examples of certain narratives and comments that circulate around chronic pain and invisible illness are:
- Why don't you ever seem to get better?
- You just need to work less and stress less.
- What's wrong with you?
- Are you going to the doctor *again*?
- Come on now, it can't be that bad...
- It must be all in your head.

People with chronic pain are often implicated as being responsible for living with pain. These judgements can come from all walks of life, from family and friends, employers and employees, practitioners, and even strangers.

Huge emotions can surface as a result of the way those with chronic pain are perceived. Not only must those with chronic pain endure the ongoing physical pain, but they also need to deal with the labels applied and the emotions that surface due to the imposed stigmas.

From personal experience, the stigmas attached to invisible illness often cause you to feel even more invisible. As a result, you feel isolated and alone in your experiences. Remember my client who was desperate to be heard and validated for his experiences while trying to get a diagnosis as opposed to trying to justify what was happening to his body and come up with reasoning to please those around him? *Psychology Today* also explored such stigmas and our 'blaming culture' and how "to be ill is to be a suspect." They look at how society perceives illness as both a reflection of the body and a person's character.[55] In reference to cancer, writer Susan Sontag stated that "much of the very reputation of the illness added to suffering of those who had it."[56]

Many individuals are not only grappling with how to manage their pain, including overhauling aspects of their lives, but they're also enduring the labels and stigmas society projects onto people with chronic pain or illness. References such as hypochondriac and attention seeker have not been lost on those experiencing pain, creating more shame and blame.

These attitudes and behaviours have caused many people (me included for a long time) to relentlessly look for ways to suppress or mask the pain, no matter the financial cost, or go against personal values, all in a desperate attempt to eliminate the pain *as well as* the shame attached to it.

While the comorbidity of chronic pain and mental health are more readily accepted now (physical symptoms and psychological symptoms increase together), we have little literature on the additional mental burden that feeling shame has on individuals. Shame and other emotions can elicit a physical reaction within the body and cause a fear response that makes us either get defensive or hide.[57] Therapists state that acute shame experiences can trigger immediate physical changes associated with a fear response, which, in turn, creates a response in the nervous system.

WHY DO WE FEEL SUCH A HUGE SENSE OF BROKENNESS AND HELPLESSNESS?

I once spoke with a psychologist who wanted to interview me for a podcast. We were discussing the types of treatments available to people, and he said that managing chronic pain isn't the role of a psychologist but rather that of a doctor or physiotherapist. It made me realise how segregated we are in treating pain. Long-term pain needs to be treated deep within both the body and the mind, and if doctors and physiotherapists don't have the tools to first investigate and then treat this, where does one go from here? Pain cannot be treated in silo.

We need to recognise that just like we as individuals have our own perception of how the world operates based on our beliefs, conditioning, upbringing and often education, so do practitioners. There are layers to these perceptions and worldviews because some practitioners work solely on the mind (psychologists and psychiatrists); others focus more on the mind, body, and spirit (psychotherapists), and others believe that trauma is stored within the body (somatic therapists). Some practitioners work in conjunction with the nervous systems, and some don't. How individual practitioners define pain is another complexity behind how they choose what treatment to recommend for you.

Society's reactions and labels attached to having an invisible illness or chronic pain disorder are the reasons why we feel like we are broken. When we hear over and over again that our body isn't working, that we're the reason why our mental health is being impacted, that we aren't coping, that our symptoms are worsening, that it's us that has the issue, it only feeds the idea that we're broken and aren't enough. This has created the rules we've been operating blindly under for too long.

It's this negative narrative and mindset that starts to embed deep within our psyche and says we aren't good enough, that we need to be fixed, and, therefore many of us live in a perpetual state of wanting to be fixed and longing for the life we had before the pain came along. This narrative isn't conducive for anyone. It creates a belief system that we're not enough with our pain, illness, and disease. It causes us to fall into scarcity, into not being enough, and, in an attempt to be enough, we start to find ways to fix ourselves. When we can't, we default into a cycle of disappointment and failure and once again think we've failed and aren't enough.

This way of thinking and behaving causes people to default into a victim mentality, leading them to isolate even more from themselves (disconnection and disassociation) and the world. This, in turn, causes even more issues (depression and anxiety), placing us at war with ourselves. This then creates a cycle of negative thoughts. Thoughts are potent and powerful, and our body hears and believes every negative or positive thought that enters the brain.

If we constantly tell our body and brain that we aren't enough, that we have failed, and that we need to be fixed, we default into a state of human 'doing' as opposed to human *being* – that is, living and experiencing the world regardless of our physical state.

So, imagine if we actually started shifting the narrative and instead of reinforcing that people aren't coping, we expressed empathy and understanding. Of course, it wouldn't be easy — how could it be?

An integrated approach is needed to teach people how to manage their pain. We must create resilience and strength within people. We need to teach them to reframe the way they see pain. We must empower people with the choices they make, and we must teach individuals to have self-compassion and how to connect back with themselves.

The truth is that we were never broken.

To break the rules of pain, you'll need you to:
- Start shifting the belief that therapists and practitioners are solely the experts.
- Start shifting the idea that we need to be validated or obtain approval.
- Understand that while practitioners are the experts in their fields, our specific needs may be outside their area of knowledge and understanding.
- Be aware of how negative energies can cause a toxic thought cycle, but we can now start taking control of this.

You're now ready to read on to Part 4 to explore the scars we carry from early trauma that create narratives we unconsciously live by, the impact of which goes on to create tension and chronic pain within the body. Get ready to unlearn what you have learnt.

Part 4

RAISED TO BELIEVE

Q. How can we truly look at and treat pain differently from what we've always believed?

A. To truly understand why the body is experiencing pain, we must delve deeper into our human makeup, psyche, and why we've learnt to behave and think the way we do.

In Part 3, we explored numerous concepts around how pain is commonly perceived and treated in this day and age. I highlighted Western medicine as having a tendency to stick to its linear approach to treating pain and how the majority of practitioners, through their beliefs and the way they treat clients, can subliminally reinforce a narrative that our bodies are somehow broken. The accepted definition of autoimmune is a prime example, in that we're told it's 'our immune systems attacking us' instead of the more constructive 'our immune system is compromised due to many different factors, causing a response that *appears* as though it's attacking the body, but the response is due to an external trigger'.

Taking small steps to support different elements of our body is the key to overall healing, implementing changes such as:

- Maintaining a good diet that helps reduce inflammation within the body.
- Making beneficial lifestyle choices every day that help both our mind, body, and spirit.
- Reducing overall stress in our life.
- Supporting our nervous system with the right environments.
- Connecting to, listening to, and acknowledging what our body requires of us each and every day.
- Focusing on reducing inflammation within our body through all of these measures.

> Over time, all of these actions will encourage your body to start repairing itself.

However, there is a widespread expectation held by so many people that to be healed means to be without pain, without symptoms, and without a compromised immune system. Holding on to this physical expectation causes many people to think that real, genuine healing is in the too-hard basket. This expectation of ourselves is also an unrealistic and impassive way of thinking about our body, and it promotes a disconnection between the body and the mind. We must remember that pain and pain symptoms are our body's way of communicating to us that it needs help.

Every day, we learn more about how complex and sophisticated the human body is. We're also beginning to understand that the way chronic pain is currently managed focuses too much on the assumption of physical causes to everything and neglects the mental and emotional pain that manifests within the physical body. The converse is also overlooked: that physical pain triggers the onset of (more) mental and emotional pain and can be a tricky cycle to unravel.

Despite any reservations you may have had, I hope you've had some of your old beliefs shaken up and have released the old perception that pain is solely negative, as this skews and narrows our approach to treatment, limits our beliefs over our body, and forever limits our healing potential.

The key questions that unlocked my understanding of real change were around why so many of us seem to harbour pain and hang on to it for so long. Why doesn't it shift?

I wanted to know:
- Why do some of us carry pain while others don't?
- Why do some of us experience pain more deeply than others?
- Why do some of us heal from pain more easily than others?

To do this, I had to go back to my childhood. I had to reflect on how I was brought into the world, how I was raised, my developmental milestones, and how these things influenced numerous constructs, beliefs, and assumptions around how I thought the world operated. In this section, I'll be delving into the psychological patterns that create our human behaviour in order for you to understand yourself, not just on a physical level but on a deeper level to break through the rules and limitations of your own pain.

STEP BACK: Therefore, I now ask that you kindly step outside and take a more objective look at yourself and your circumstances to observe yourself using a bird's-eye perspective. This requires you to detach and separate yourself from the physical pain your body feels, but don't forget to come back to yourself! We don't want you to remain detached but instead to become an observer of yourself, your body, and your life.

It even requires you to take a step back from the conscious awareness you're used to. You must become conscious of your consciousness.

Once we objectively understand how humans behave in relation to chronic pain, we can look back introspectively and with compassion at our previous selves, who didn't know better, and this new awareness starts creating change. You can call this an awakening if you like. I think of it as opening a once-lost temple that contains a vast number of discoveries and insights about *your* individual human body.

While reducing the symptoms has always been crucial for me, the most fundamental element in all of this is learning about the person I am and accepting myself wholly and fully, regardless of what's happening within my internal body.

Some people's key turning points in life revolve around a near-death or life-altering experience, and many talk of an out-of-body experience that becomes an epiphany about how their existence relates to the world they thought they knew. The epiphany shows them something about human consciousness and their significance in relation to this.

For me, there was no one 'aha' moment or significant moment, but rather a number of difficult lessons that gave me profound insight into how I needed to change my life to let in healing, change, and growth and become the person I am today. It's these lessons that are pivotal in providing the change and evolution we require.

THERE IS NO MAGIC PILL

I won't lie – sometimes the journey has been painstakingly slow and arduous. At times, I've wished for a different life story, but I also know that I would have never approached life the way I have without somewhat being forced to. If it weren't for my challenging experiences, I wouldn't be where I am today. Living with and experiencing chronic pain has enabled me to create a strength, a resilience, and an appreciation for my body that I've never felt before. As I feel my body heal and release the pain, I know that everything I discuss works. I'm living proof of this.

But I need to set something straight: there's no magic pill to fix you, to cure you, to heal you, or to take away your pain. I wish there were – I really do – but if there were, there wouldn't be the opportunity for you to do this inward journey where you'll discover how amazing your body is and how amazing your life as a human is. It is those very challenges that make you extraordinary.

But there is no magic pill or Prince Charming!

> **Q. Why do I need to tell you this?**
>
> A. Because for so many of us, as early as we can remember, we were exposed to this notion of fairytales, where there was a princess (and even these days, a prince) in distress. A charming prince would ride along, rescue the princess, and kiss her; normality would be restored, and they would go and live happily ever after.

This story, this narrative, is something many of us have been fed as children. Many of us, especially females, have been waiting our entire lives for our Prince Charming to arrive on his horse and save us, provide for us, and even whisk us away to a better life or existence. That prince charming could be in the form of a doctor, a specialist, someone whom we are in relationship with – the list goes on. This means we sit in a period of stagnation for weeks, months, even years… waiting for someone to rescue us. We've deflected responsibility and placed the onus on someone else.

Many men out there carry the belief that they're responsible for saving their female counterparts. Because of this, they carry an added responsibility, which can add enormous pressure if they already experience chronic pain.

We must put to bed that old notion that good things come to those who wait. So many people are sitting and waiting while doing nothing to help themselves move forward. To be able to achieve the physical healing we require, we need to take action. Sitting stagnant doesn't serve us. We must peel back the layers of our lives to see what's at the core and rebuild ourselves from the inside out.

It's time to dispel some old fairytales that are no longer relevant.

- You have the power within you.
- Your survival and existence aren't reliant upon someone saving you.
- As a man, you don't need to continue to take on old gender stereotypes to prove your worth.
- As a woman, you don't need to wait for a man or a prince charming to rescue you.
- Your happiness isn't dependent upon someone else. It's solely dependent upon you and the choices you make to move forward in your life.
- Again, the power lies within you. It always has.

REVEALING YOUR CORE ESSENCE

Let's rewire the notion of healing by removing the undue pressure that society places on us to heal and become whole and free of disease. While being free of disease and without pain is most people's intent, some of us may never fully be free of pain, and **that is okay.** Constantly trying to resist this is exhausting. Accepting this has the power to lessen the pain.

For many with autoimmunity and pain, our risk of experiencing symptoms is higher than the 'average' person. But does this mean we're incomplete or not whole? No. This narrative is subtly injected into society, causing guilt and shame within those who experience pain, but this doesn't serve anyone at all. Our own misplaced expectations and those of other people who claim we should be free of symptoms or free of disease should not define our worth: **healing is so much more than this.**

Healing is coming to a place full of acceptance for the individual you are today and understanding who you are fundamentally without all the external noise telling you who you are or whom you need to be and validating yourself based upon this. To achieve this, you must peel back all the layers that have made you who you are today.

Like an onion, we are made up of many things we've learnt and been exposed to over our lifetime. Our inner self is the very core of that onion. It is our divine self, the one born into this world in our purest form.

The layers of the onion gradually build up as we become exposed to the different ways of the world, which we, in turn, categorise as good and bad, such as:

- Experiencing emotions like heartache and disappointment
- People's reactions affecting our sense of wellbeing
- Different thought processes
- Different values and beliefs
- Different ways of thinking
- Our parents' expectations of us

- Different parenting styles
- Different styles of attachment
- Different upbringings
- Societal expectations
- Experiencing traumas… and the list goes on and on.

The layers build up around our core (pure self); over time, we become influenced by them in addition to society's way of living and doing. All these layers create our individual self and influence how we view the world. We carry memories and imprints within our conscious and subconscious; these wounds, these scars underpin how we think, behave, feel, and act as adults.

Reflection: Our pain may sit overarching all these layers, or it may be interspersed between them.

Healing is removing all these layers to enable us to return to ourselves, our pure and unique core that makes us different from any other person in the world. This has been referred to as *unlearning* everything we've learnt over the years. This not only means identifying all the constructs that have made us who we are but also the rules and conditions that have been imposed on us or that we've imposed on ourselves because of how we've been raised. These constructs and rules have prevented us from moving forward and breaking through some of the barriers of our pain.

Removing these layers and these constructs means knowing, first of all, that we are not broken and do not need to be fixed. If you do not deeply believe this, you will always struggle against healing.

Healing prompt: #You are not broken.

Kintsugi, also known as kintsukuroi, is the beautiful, ancient Japanese art form of repairing broken ceramics with gold to make them stronger and even more beautiful than they were originally. Instead of discarding the broken pieces, they place them into position with gold inlay, which is thought to add significance and beauty by drawing attention to the weaknesses and showing that reforming where it was broken makes it stronger than before; the break becomes the cornerstone of the whole piece.

Imagine if we could use this same analogy within our everyday life. Imagine if all the bits that we thought were broken, all our trauma and life experiences, the hardships and the fears were actually the nuggets of gold that provided us light and propelled us forward to see our absolute true potential. Imagine if they were the aspects that cemented and moulded us together.

Imagine if we could use this same analogy for our body and instead of dismissing the broken parts, we could see beauty in these aspects instead of thinking they were flaws. Ultimately, the challenges that propel us deep down into the depths of darkness are the catalyst for us to create change in order to see the light.

Healing prompt: #Accept yourself, just as you are – right now. Let go.

> Healing is returning to our body.

Healing is learning to stop attacking ourselves, consciously and subconsciously. Instead of criticising and fighting ourselves and the world, we need to take a step back and learn to accept who we are, battle wounds, scars and all. This is all part of the human experience, after all.

But where did our inner battles first begin? Let's delve into our pivotal entry into the world and the constructs that framed us as individuals.

EARLY CONSTRUCTS DEVELOPED IN CHILDHOOD

It's crucial to understand that our early development underpins why so many of us carry hidden stress within the body as adults. This stress results in physical symptoms and, over a prolonged period, becomes chronic. While you look for causes in your current life, often it all stems back to an earlier time in your life.

Beginning with our most basic needs to survive and then grow and develop, in the 1940s, the prominent psychologist Abraham Maslow explored human motivation and cognition and created a five-tier model of human needs, depicted with five hierarchical levels within a pyramid.

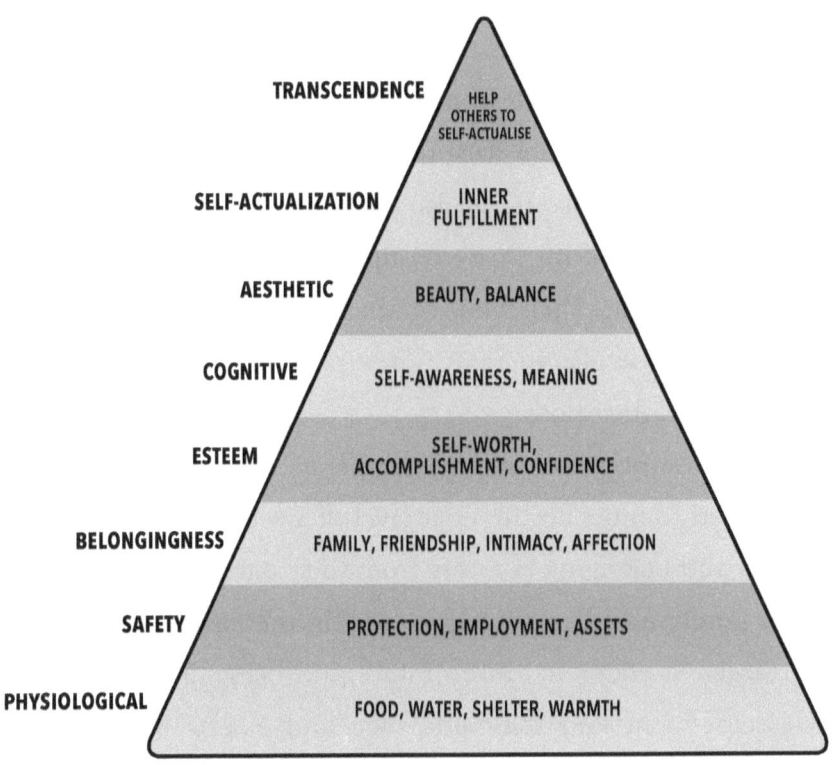

Maslow's Pyramid

Maslow believed that as our needs within each level are met, the motivation to meet that need decreases, and we move to the next level (or motivation) of needs to be fulfilled. At the bottom of the pyramid are our most basic primal needs. He referred to these as our physiological needs in the form of air, water, food, shelter, and sleep.

Once we achieve these, we move on to the next level of needs, which are safety needs. As children, we need to achieve a sense of safety and security within our immediate environment to know that the world is a safe place. For example, from birth, a baby determines whether or not they can obtain their most basic physical and emotional needs from their parents or caretakers. If the baby can, they will gain trust in the caregivers, creating a sense of safety and security. If this isn't achieved or felt, the baby will maintain a sense of mistrust over those who care for them, which goes on to impact their view of the world. As the baby grows, this mistrust will also influence their perception of how to trust themself and their body.

If a sense of safety and security is achieved, the individual is believed to move to the next level of needs, which is a sense of love and belonging not only from their parents but also from other family members and those within the community. When we receive a concrete sense of love and belonging, this builds our self-esteem and self-confidence and asserts firm boundaries in order for us to feel respected by others. This respect feeds into our ability to self-actualise, which means realising our potential within the world. It enables full acceptance of ourselves and finding fulfilment through positive purpose or creative expression.

PART 4

Q. What happens to individuals whose needs are not met at each level? For those children who were raised in insecure, abusive, or volatile environments where they didn't receive the security a child needs to know that they're safe in this world, how does this threaten their sense of security in the wider world?

A. To answer from my own experience, living in an orphanage for the first five years of my life meant that my physiological needs were challenged. Although I did have food, shelter, water, clothing, and sleep, they were limited, and my inner being knew this. Not knowing when I would receive food, love, care, hugs, water, and sleep caused me to be always on guard and hypervigilant. This hyper-state impacted my sense of safety and security within the world, where I didn't know who I could rely on and trust. I knew deep down that I yearned to be loved, and because this need went unmet for so long, I came to believe that I was unworthy of existing and unworthy of being loved and cared for.

Much work is being done to learn more about the impact of developmental trauma on creating stress within the body. Positive childhood development is so significant in the development of one's sense of self. In order to have a concrete sense of self, you need to have had your formative childhood needs met because their presence, or lack thereof, will strongly influence how the brain and the body develop and function as you grow, continuing to influence the body as an adult.

While we still tend to think of and define trauma as actual physical or mental abuse, growing research has found that a child doesn't need to have been abused to suffer trauma or mental scarring. In fact, the child only needs to *perceive* the abuse and experience being abandoned in some way by a primary caregiver to be strongly affected in the longer term.

Many individuals who I've worked with were raised in a loving environment, but there were still moments where this was challenged:

- The absent father
- The alcoholic parent
- The motherless mother who didn't know how to mother because she wasn't mothered herself
- The mother who didn't know how to praise and affirm her kids in the manner they required.

We have talked about intergenerational trauma briefly, and here we can affirm again that it comes in many forms. For example, if our parents, out of their own long-held fears, subconsciously projected their fears onto us and didn't give us a strong sense of confidence, support, and autonomy to explore our world, this can create a sense of failure and feelings of shame and doubt about our own world and ourselves.

If children aren't given the skills to acquire a strong sense of power, this can influence their entire lives. It can also impact how they continue to go through each additional stage of development, reducing the potential pathways open to them. Strong constructs and limitations can predetermine their mindset, which can become more and more set and skewed. Somewhere in their development, a seed is planted about a story or a belief system that underpins who they are today.

Reflection Exercise:
Can you take a step back, look at yourself objectively, and find the developmental seed of how you became who you are today?

For many of us who experience chronic, debilitating pain, we've had to overhaul many significant aspects of our lives. For some, it has meant a loss of livelihood, a loss of income, and a loss of safety and security. For some again, even our basic physiological needs, such as the ability to sleep, can be challenged. When we refer back to the hierarchy of needs, we can now start to see how our sense of safety and security may be challenged if we can no longer work because of physical limitations and fatigue. This negatively impacts our sense of belonging to our social structures and community. This, in turn, causes us to withdraw further, and, because of this, we feel unworthy and lacking in love, which contributes to the chronic pain we feel.

PSYCHOSOCIAL FACTORS IN DEVELOPMENT

Another prominent theory in understanding human behaviour and personality development is psychosocial theory. Psychosocial theory looks at how the combination of psychological factors and one's social environment impact mental and emotional wellbeing to shape an individual into the person they become.

There are eight stages to the development of an individual, beginning at birth and ending at death. Each state is usually identified by a goal. It will also impact how they continue to go through each additional stage and predetermine how they operate within the world and venture through the remaining stages of life.

It is believed that our life is largely based upon the choices we make at each stage.[1] Yet remember, this ties in with Maslow's hierarchy of firstly achieving a sense of safety and security with our most primal physiological needs. If we don't fulfil our most basic primal needs, we may miss out on developing key skills and resources to evolve in such a way to achieve our absolute potential.

- 0–1 years of age: Where basic trust is achieved. A child will determine whether or not they'll be able to trust the world based upon whether or not they receive their most basic physiological needs and achieve a sense of love and belonging.
- 1–3 years of age: Where autonomy and the ability to achieve basic tasks occur. If we had parents who were overly concerned about us hurting ourselves and didn't allow us enough independence to walk, run, fall, and touch things, it smothers our sense of autonomy and our rightful place in the world due to the projection of our parents' fears onto us.

These fears could also create an individual who is hypervigilant and hypersensitive to their environment, always on guard, waiting for something bad to happen, a sense that can follow them throughout their lives. If children aren't given the skills to acquire a strong sense of their own power and ability to navigate the world, this can diminish their innate potential throughout their lives.

You can see now that each of us is a by-product of our upbringing, and these theories can help us understand the constructs behind how we operate within the world.

AFFIRMING BEHAVIOURS AND ASSIGNING GOOD AND BAD

When we look at human behaviour and how we're motivated

to behave, most of it is based upon positive reinforcement and praise. I've often had this discussion with my mum that raising a baby or child is really no different from raising and training a dog.

"What?!" I hear you say. But wait – hear me out.

When dogs are trained, they undertake strict training where a trainer uses positive reinforcement to encourage the animal to do whatever is asked of it through commands. When the dog displays the desired behaviour, we reinforce the behaviour by providing it with praise or a reward (treat). When the dog disobeys or does not undertake the desired behaviour, we use punishment to reinforce that this is not the behaviour we want it to undertake.

This type of reinforcement and association is what behavioural psychologists refer to as 'conditioning'. As humans, we use conditioning frequently in our everyday interactions. We use love, praise, and affirmation to encourage the desired behaviour, and we withhold them to discourage undesired behaviour. From an early age, our behaviour becomes 'conditioned', meaning that to get the love, praise, and affirmation we desire, there are conditions to be met – and it starts early in life.

For parents with young children, how often do you get asked, "Is your baby a good baby?" Meaning, does your baby feed well, or is it a fussy eater? Do they sleep well, or do they not sleep through the night? Does this mean that all the babies who don't sleep well or have difficulty feeding are 'bad' babies? Let's continue on this trajectory.

If you're a parent, when you were encouraging your baby or infant to roll over, to crawl, to walk, did you do so by saying 'good girl' (or 'good boy')? While it's subtle, we're still teaching and conditioning our kids to perform in a certain manner to receive recognition from us. We're also teaching them that certain behaviour equates to being perceived as 'good', and if they aren't good, it implies that they are bad. As babies and infants, we're taught that so much of other people's love, acceptance, and approval is driven by certain behaviours; therefore, we learn to respond to certain cues.

The terminology we use teaches parents and their children that performance is based upon criteria. If children adhere to these expectations (feed well, maintain a good weight, sleep well, no colic or reflux, not fussy), we label them as good. If they don't achieve those things, they are bad. We fail to recognise that all babies are good babies and all babies are meant to sleep and cry. Instead, we categorise them as good or bad.

As children and teenagers, this narrative of not being enough is spread through mass and social media and even our community without knowing it. How many of us can look back on our childhood years where we were told (or it was implied) that we were not enough, not pretty enough, skinny enough, popular enough, rich enough? Just look at the extent to which print and digital media marketing abuses our insecurities and exploits them in order to sell a product we don't need. **All of these subtle messages accumulate over time to create a culture where we believe we aren't enough.**

This mindset and narrative are often extended and carried through our adolescence by our parents and our teachers, and we believe we need to achieve to amount to anything. We often grow up in a system that benchmarks us based upon our academia, and if we deviate from the norm or are 'underachievers', then it's heavily implied that we won't succeed in life.

Creative types struggle with this notion because we've been taught that academia sets us up for success. Once again, we feel like we aren't enough or we don't fit in within the 'norm' or we won't succeed, so we abort our sense of creativity to achieve a sense of belonging that society has taught us we need. Many of us have been conditioned by different role models to receive praise, validation, love, and so on, and we continue to seek it, from childhood, throughout adolescence, and all the way to adulthood.

Q. What happens when we can no longer partake in the behaviour that provides us with that praise, love, and validation?

A. Our human conditioning is activated, and we tell ourselves we aren't enough and we can't achieve what we want to achieve. We, in turn, project blame onto ourselves.

When we hold the underlying belief that we aren't enough, it sits dormant within our subconscious and impacts our lives each day. If we delve deep enough, it goes back as far as gender stereotype roles when women demonstrated worth by being at home, fulfilling their duties as a housewife and ensuring that everything was taken care of to give the hardworking man every creature comfort. The man, on the other hand, was expected to provide for his family with long hours and no emotional support. If men and women deviated from these roles, they were judged harshly.

As a female growing up in generation X, where multiculturalism was a thing of the future, I lived in a time when cultures and races didn't blend, so, being a Chinese girl within a Caucasian family, I stood out. From day one, I knew I was different from the blonde girls with white skin, with my dark hair, almond-shaped eyes, and different skin tone. I looked different; I felt different; I didn't have a strong sense of who I was in a world that constantly marketed and reinforced that I wasn't enough.

This continued throughout my life in the way I parented and the way I held myself, constantly influenced by subliminal messaging, marketing, and clever product placement that reinforced the belief that I wasn't enough. My looks weren't enough; my education wasn't enough; my goals weren't enough; my career progression wasn't enough. I needed to be more, earn more, achieve more.

So, I pushed and strived to be enough in a culture where I would never be enough, all while my body was breaking under the pressure of it all.

When I was diagnosed with fibromyalgia, I was parenting a 6-month-old while looking after my 4-year-old, trying to hold down a part-time job in corporate IT, and attempting postgraduate studies. I was so close to burnout but lived in a culture that reinforced that if I wanted it all, I needed to continue to work and strive for it. How many times have we heard that women can have it all? For men nowadays, sharing the load of parenting and working can also generate the same unmanageable pressure.

For many of us, we believe we can have it all, but at what cost to our body and our health? This narrative is feeding into a culture where we're experiencing more and more burnout, mental health concerns, anxiety, and loneliness alongside an increase in health conditions.

Q. How does this build up into chronic pain?

A. When our body starts to ask us to slow down through fatigue, health conditions, or imbalances, or when we start to feel disconnected, our conditioning causes us to believe we aren't good enough. We then project blame onto ourselves and our body for not adhering to society's expectations or our own expectations of how we believe we need to perform in order to be approved of. As a result, we feel like failures.

Our lack of worth will be further reinforced if we can't partake in the activities we used to. Loss of independence, loss of freedom, and loss of physical ability create a huge sense of failure.

When we can't engage in social situations or if our health limits us from social activities that created connection and gave us love and validation, we start to internalise the narrative that we aren't good enough (more pressure). Many of us will try to overcompensate and push ourselves further to prove to ourselves and others that we are worthy.

THE IMPACT OF WORDS AND PHRASES ON OUR CONDITIONING

Let's take this one step further and look at the impact that certain words and phrases have had on our conditioning and how this has impacted modern human culture.

Emotions are a crucial part of the human experience. Emotions are felt within the body and elicit a physiological response. As children, many of us were taught that certain emotions, such as anger, rage, fear, shock, frustration, sadness, and disgust, are bad and should not be expressed, so we learnt to repress them.

I often think of the odd adage that children should be seen and not heard. For children raised in my era, we often heard such references and learnt quickly that children were to be seen, to be on show, to act right, to sit and stay still. Tantrums reflected a parent's inability to control or parent their child or implied that the child was 'naughty'.

There were many other detrimental phrases, such as:
- "Don't be silly," when children tried to show emotion or express themselves strongly.
- "Toughen up," which implied to not show any weakness.
- "Don't be a girl" or "Stop acting like a girl," which implied that girls were physically and emotionally weaker and was said to any boy who expressed 'feminine' emotions, as doing so was deemed socially unacceptable.

Mine was a generation where so many references and assumptions were assigned to these labels. The result of this has been a generation of adults who have grown up to believe they can't express themselves out of fear of being labelled 'outspoken' and 'bad'. Instead, they learnt to shut off these emotions to prevent shame and rejection, yet they weren't taught nor given the environment to acquire skills to manage and effectively express negative emotions.[2] They subsequently acquired a sense of helplessness, sometimes unconsciously.

This helplessness, whether perceived or real, is a potential trigger for a biological stress response, which can create physiological changes in the body.

For example, each time an individual encounters an experience that triggers an emotion, their inability to know how to deal with this creates a stress response that, in turn, activates the parasympathetic nervous system to alert the body that there is a threat. The person soon learns that they must do everything they can to avoid such a threat.[3]

While it varies within individuals, it's apparent that there's a generation of individuals disconnected from themselves and their innermost being due to old parenting standards and a society that taught them it was bad and not socially acceptable to be themselves, to express emotions or thoughts, to be heard or to be seen. **As a survival mechanism, they learnt to disconnect and reject the aspects of themselves they deemed unacceptable.**

Exercise:

Over the next few weeks, as you keep returning to the passages in this book, take the time to reflect on your childhood, adolescence, and even your adult life, the times when you thought that you weren't enough. These moments could include: not getting the approval of your parents, not getting the approval from your teachers, not being accepted into a team, not being approved by a certain social group, not feeling accepted by someone you were interested in, not getting into an institution, or not getting a job offer. With each of these, I would like you to delve a little deeper and think about the feelings you embodied during these experiences and the narrative you spoke over yourself.

This exercise is particularly useful in identifying how we create constructs and stories and project blame onto ourselves for situations that are beyond our control. It also highlights how unmet needs and emotions often stem from a very early age and continue replicating until they're acknowledged and met. See if you can come from a place of compassion and start to meet the parts of yourself that you felt weren't good enough with words of love.

ANGER AND THE MANIFESTATION OF CHRONIC PAIN

John E Sarno, MD and author of *The Mind Body Prescription*, explores contained emotions further and believes that such emotions as fear, anxiety, and depression aren't linked to the manifestation of chronic pain. John believes that the underlying culprit is suppressed anger that leads to a "reservoir of rage within the unconscious mind."[4] **He has discovered that repressed anger and rage can be a direct contributor to pain disorders.**

Sarno believes that three factors come into play:

1. Internal conflict within oneself
2. The stresses and strains of daily life
3. The residue of anger and rage from one's infancy and childhood

HOW TO WORK WITH THE FULL SPECTRUM OF EMOTIONS

Dr Russ Harris, MD, a psychologist and author of *The Happiness Trap*, uses a particular line of therapy called acceptance and commitment therapy (ACT) to help individuals work through painful thoughts and feelings to create a rich and meaningful life.[5] To do this, we must look at and understand our programming and how we've been taught to perceive certain emotions. When we look at chronic pain, I believe we need to apply a similar approach, examining how we've been taught to perceive our body as either good or bad, what emotions surface when we perceive our body to be functioning (good) or not functioning (bad), and, in turn, what thoughts and emotions about ourselves arise because of this.

The following phrases may be relatable to those with chronic pain:

- I can't talk about my pain because it's a sign of weakness.
- I am weak if I show that I am in pain.
- I am not allowed to be angry.
- Showing mental vulnerability is a sign of weakness.
- There must be something wrong with me because I am not coping.
- I can't talk about my pain because people will judge me for having pain in my body.
- I must have done something wrong.
- I am responsible for my pain.
- My pain isn't shifting; therefore, I must be at fault.
- What is wrong with me?
- Why me?

All of these questions and scenarios feed into the part of our brain that keeps telling us we aren't worthy or good enough, and we continue on this feedback loop, unable to get off that train that keeps increasing in speed and perpetually cycling these thoughts. Somewhere in our upbringing, we've inherited the belief that we can only show up when we're well, and if we aren't well, we can't show up because we aren't acceptable to society, which once again feeds into this notion that we mustn't even be acceptable to ourselves.

Some deep questions to answer are:
- How do you think you need to show up in front of your colleagues, in front of your family, and in front of your friends?
- Do you find that you need to alter yourself or who you are to conform to others' expectations?
- Do you think people accept you as you are?
- Do you feel that you need to 'mask' your emotions and put on a positive and happy disposition?
- What emotions rise within you when you don't feel accepted?
- How does it feel inside when you can't express yourself?
- What emotions tend to arise when you feel that you can't express yourself? What do you do with these emotions?

When working with clients, answering these questions is a pivotal moment in understanding how they've created negative and positive associations with their thoughts and emotions, especially in reference to the effect on the body. My work with clients also looks at particular gender stereotypical roles that we've inherited across our lifetime. These can impact our ability to allow others to help us, and this resistance has a flow-on effect on our body and our ability to heal.

WHEN THOUGHTS BECOME REALITY

When you have a recurring thought, it creates a belief. When you start to accept this belief as truth, it shifts from your conscious awareness into your subconscious awareness and underpins who you are, even though it only started as a thought.

If we haven't been taught how to process emotional responses within us, the most vulnerable aspects of ourselves are triggered and become all we can focus on. These thoughts turn into beliefs and infiltrate our conscious mind, our subconscious mind, our energetic field, and our physical body, and we start to house these criticisms as truths.

This is essentially what the law of attraction is. When we think we aren't worthy or good enough, these thoughts take up more and more space within our minds and replace any good feelings and thoughts. Fixating on these thoughts soon starts to engulf our reality. These thoughts become us, and we become these thoughts. We let them define who we are, and we become stuck in that way of thinking, living, and being.

We become stuck between a rock and a hard place.

People become trapped in ways of behaving, within lifestyles and even within their physical bodies, unable to make change because of the perceived threat that the change will result in shame. Shame is the "intensely painful feeling or experience of believing that we are flawed and therefore unworthy of love and belonging – something we've experienced, done, or failed to do makes us unworthy of connection."[6]

This is how we, as people with chronic pain, become stuck, struggling to look beyond the situation. Because of the shame, we feel attached to:

- Having a diagnosis
- Our body's inability to function how we expect it to
- Losing independence over our physical body
- Having to ask for help
- Not being able to engage in activities we once did
- Not being able to partake in our existing life.

Becoming stuck in this way of thinking only creates more mental anguish and turmoil and results in more 'negative emotions' that we then try to push away.

The by-product of shame is guilt. Shame is about the self, for example, when a person feels bad about themselves because of how they've been mistreated. Guilt, however, occurs when a person feels bad about their behaviour.[7] Shame and guilt are two prominent emotions when it comes to chronic pain. Both have a huge mental impact, keeping people trapped and stuck, and toxic positivity has caused many of us to feel shame and guilt for experiencing shame and guilt. There needs to come a time when we can meet these two emotions with compassion and curiosity instead of judgement, understanding that both have arisen because of our conditioning, our experiences, and so forth. Relinquishing negative attachments to shame and guilt is a beautiful step in moving forward on your healing journey.

Healing prompt: #It's time to say farewell to shame and guilt.

When it comes to chronic illness, there is a growing belief that is being marketed by many different corners of the world: we can heal naturally from disease, and our body has the innate wisdom to be able to do so. While I most definitely believe that there is truth to this, I also believe that this particular mindset and this narrative can be detrimental to the masses of people who may need Western medicine intervention and sometimes prescription medicine.

While I do believe there is a culture of over-reliance on prescription and Western medicine, I also believe there is a time and place where prescription medicine is required, for example:

- When people don't have access to other integrated therapies.
- If they cannot afford these additional therapies.
- If their body and brain simply need a break from the chronic aspect of their pain or illness.

While I don't personally believe long-term use of any prescription medicine is beneficial for our overall body, we shouldn't guilt people for their choices. Instead, we can empower them with knowledge and options. Imposing our belief system not to use prescription medicine can provide those with chronic illness with even more of a sense of failure, setting them up further for disappointment and failure, which in turn can alienate them further.

Similarly, we shouldn't judge those who opt for the more natural alternatives to support their body. Each individual knows their body and values the best.

MAKING A CONSCIOUS CHOICE TO MOVE FORWARD

We are all experiencing hardships, all experiencing different forms of the human experience. For some, this may manifest as physical pain and disease; for others, it may result in financial hardship; for others again, it may be loss and grief. Regardless, the day will come when we're given a choice to either move forward from the internal pain and the hardships, starting the inner work to release some of the pain we're carrying, or to carry it for the rest of our lives.

> "As you find the light in you, you begin to see the light in everyone else."
> – Ram Dass

Healing prompt: #Acceptance doesn't mean failure.

Now we're realising how much repressed emotions impact the overall functioning of our body and especially how much repressed anger contributes to the manifestation of pain. Similarly, when it comes to experiencing pain within our body, it's our automatic default to fight it. Our brain sends a signal to tell our entire body that it's in pain, and, similar to a stress response, our body activates the parasympathetic nervous system, which in turn floods the body with cortisol and shuts down other parts of the body, ready to fight, flee, or freeze.

In our case, though, when the pain is long-term and chronic, it means that our body is in a continual state of fighting the pain. Continually fighting our pain actually means that we're fighting ourselves each and every day. It causes us to become hypervigilant, continually bracing for the pain to return or the next flare-up. This soon becomes our default, and our brain and body burn themselves out. Contrary to what so many people will tell you, fighting your pain isn't conducive to your body in the long term for this exact reason. When we fight, there's resistance to the situation along with resistance to ourselves and what's occurring within us. When we don't have acceptance, we allow the emotions, the anger, the fighting, and the resistance to become prolonged and even more chronic.

When you learn to come to a place of acceptance, it means you're able to accept yourself and your situation, as you are, at any given point, with kindness and compassion. Although the pain may still be there, you start to see yourself in a different light.

Instead of reacting to what's occurring within your body with anger, rage, and disdain, instead of defaulting into comparison or the victim mentality, instead of thinking you aren't enough and falling into self-judgement, you learn to set that aside and say, "I see you, and I love and accept you as you are." Over time, you can come to a place of acceptance and observe your experiences objectively, asking why they're occurring.

This is how you start to break the stronghold. Instead of focusing solely on the negativity, you can shift your focus to how you can support your body while also focusing on the positive things in your life.

Acceptance by no means equates to failure. It means accepting yourself as you are right now. It means no longer fighting yourself; it means no longer bracing for something bad to occur; it means no longer being in a hypervigilant state, ready for the worst outcome. It means gently tending to your body and allowing it deep rest. It means no longer being at war with yourself but coming from a place of deep compassion. It means finding gratitude in the aspects of your life and body that are amazing and positive, such as the ability to move, breathe, wake up, and make decisions. It means redirecting your time and energy to choices that benefit you as opposed to limiting you

Healing prompt: #You no longer need to be afraid of your pain.
Physical pain can cause a whirlwind of mental and emotional pain. It can weigh us down. It can distort perceptions and cause

us to question ourselves, our body, and the world we live in, but more than anything, it can keep us in a state of fear.

Alan Gordon, founder and director of the Pain Psychology Center and author of *The Way Out*, talks about the Pain Fear Cycle, a feedback loop in which pain creates a fear response, which in turn creates more pain, which causes neuroplastic pain to become chronic.

1. The pain within our body creates fear. This could be fear attached to the unknown, fear of uncertainty within the body, fear of not being seen, fear of not doing enough, fear of not being enough, fear of not healing, fear of never being 'normal'.
2. The fear puts the brain on high alert.
3. Which leads to more fear.

Which leads to more pain.[8]

The more we become afraid of our pain, whether physical, emotional, or mental, the more we're likely to become stuck, and each time the symptom of pain arises, a fear response will be initiated. What's crucial is learning not only how to address the fears but also what underlies them.

For many clients I've worked with, the fear attaches to the fear of the unknown, the fear of uncertainty within the body, the fear of the pain never leaving, the fear of never being 'normal'. Underlying these fears are the fear of not being seen like they once were, the fear of not doing enough, the fear of not being enough, the fear of not being accepted. Even underlying these fears is the fear of being isolated because of what's happening to their internal body, which prevents them from engaging in activities that allow them to feel a sense of community, belonging, being loved, and being accepted. This leads back to childhood development phases and potential unmet needs.

UNMET CHILDHOOD NEEDS

When we look at childhood, we can look back to determine whether or not we had our needs met within important categories and, if they weren't, in what capacity they may have influenced our ability to reach the next stage.

As a child, I developed a construct where I believed that those who grew up in an orphanage were unloved and unwanted, and anyone who grew up in a normal family was loved and wanted. I set up my entire existence believing I wasn't enough. It was established so deep within my subconscious that this recurring thought soon became my reality. Because I believed I wasn't good enough, I did everything to prove I was.

As I reflect, I often think about all the times I felt I wasn't enough. I came to the realisation that maybe the majority of us wouldn't be trying to fill so many voids that we perceive are within us if we started to identify and meet the needs that weren't met in childhood.

Because of this, many adults are walking around as traumatised kids who have closed themselves off to the world and to others as a protective mechanism and to avoid getting hurt. Add to that trauma all the additional stressors and life experiences, and you can start to understand why many of us have nervous systems that are totally over-wired and frazzled and no longer know how to regulate themselves.

Going back and recognising what needs may not have been met while we were children, reversing the stories, the association, and the narratives that we imposed upon ourselves and providing us with empowered narratives is extremely impactful in helping to heal, guide, and empower our adult self.

LEARNING TO NOT JUST LOVE OURSELVES BUT TO LIKE OURSELVES

When we hold up a mirror to society, it shows us the endless number of subliminal messages telling us we aren't good enough. Yet, we're in a new age now where we know the truth – mass marketing psychology put aside for the moment – that we absolutely are good enough exactly as we are.

Many people have been on the receiving end of conditional love and approval, and also disappointment; life comes with both experiences. The sad reality is that most people could easily tell you 20 things they dislike about themselves, but rarely could these same people tell you 20 things they like about themselves. Sad, isn't it?

I ultimately believe that healing isn't just returning to the person you were born to be but also learning how to like and love yourself without the conditions that society and others impose upon you. It's going back to the basics, learning about who you are and developing a relationship with this person. It's developing the key foundations you need for any relationship, such as trust and patience, and then learning how to build upon them over time until you learn to love yourself. Like any relationship, there are often barriers, such as mental barriers and heart barriers, that want to protect us from exposing ourselves or being too vulnerable for fear of being hurt. You may have to forgive yourself numerous times for words spoken over yourself, for the heartache you've endured, for choices that weren't the best, or for not being kind to yourself. Being in a relationship with yourself takes commitment. Just like anything, plant the seed and water it, and soon you'll see your relationship with yourself start to grow and flourish.

PS – after reading this, please take the time to write a list of the things you like about yourself and see if you can expand on this list every day.

Healing prompt: #It's time to put yourself and your needs before everyone else.

There's an argument that somehow putting ourselves first and considering our needs is selfish. So many of us have been raised to be selfless, to always think of others before ourselves. Our upbringing has created a belief that focusing on ourselves and our lives is selfish. In addition, social conditioning causes us to think that we need to take on the burden and responsibility of others as well as carrying our own load, but the truth is, we don't.

The only person we can be responsible for is ourselves. We believe we're broke, and because of this, we walk around trying to fix others and heal them, but, in doing so, we neglect ourselves and our needs, all while trying to be the good partner, the good wife, the good mother, the good employee, when all of this continually places even more pressure on ourselves and our body.

Doing the work is hard, and it hurts like hell!!

Rarely do we look at how courageous it is to do the work. Without a doubt, it's hard to go inwards, to discover that so much of who we are is a by-product of our environment and the way we were raised. While this can be confronting for many of us (if not all of us), we need to be cognisant not to project blame on our parents or our caretakers, as they too were simply a by-product of their own upbringing and environment.

This can give us solace that it isn't our fault – it never was – but now that you have this conscious awareness, to sit and ignore it would mean that you're adding to the problem instead of creating a shift.

Most of us haven't been taught to do the hard learning; we haven't been taught to confront the aspects of ourselves that we may not like; we haven't been told that it's okay to have emotions, to cry, to be ourselves. We need to start peeling back the layers and identifying who we really are.

All the emotions, all the hurt, all the pain is sitting within us, wanting to be acknowledged, wanting to be heard. It is simply this: once we have the courage to sit with all of this, to sit with ourselves and allow everything to be heard, we can shift our mindset and our pain.

In Part 5, the final section of this book, we will explore the power of integrative healing through the four pillars of disrupting pain. As you read on, I want you to think about the story you tell yourself about your situation and whether it limits or liberates you. Ultimately, it's *your* story, and you get to decide how it plays out.

Part 5

INTEGRATED HEALING

I'm excited to now present to you my key principles of Integrated Healing.

For many people, finding freedom will require moving out of a strictly traditional medical model (that is, placing all expectations on external practitioners to fix you) and instead listening carefully for the first time to your body's needs and intuitively connecting with it. This means actually learning and deciphering what your body requires of you in order to support it at any given time. If your body talks, you'll learn to listen and respond accordingly to support yourself.

I hope that learning about all of the unconscious limitations you may place upon yourself has been truly insightful and empowering enough for you to know that you have the power to shift them, as this is how you create change within your life. It's the only way to take ownership of your healing, regain your power, and stop relying on external fixes to make you feel better.

An important note – this doesn't mean not leveraging your team of practitioners to guide and support you. They're fundamental, as is support from your community. However, instead of having this underlying belief that you require them to fix and heal you, your relationship with them will start to come from a place where you know that your body has the ability to heal itself. Your body is facilitating all of this with their help, guidance, and particular expertise.

Finally, the cream on top is to change the narrative to state that regardless of your health condition, you can live a life with purpose and fulfilment, not dictated by pain. Your body and what's happening within you internally doesn't define who you are. You are the embodiment of so much more. I live my life by this, and you will, too.

From this point forward, you will take ownership of your health, with you and your body co-creating what it requires to heal and thrive. It's time to turn the old narrative around that our body isn't working for us when, in fact, she is our biggest ally, upholding us, literally carrying us and supporting us each and every day! It's time to relinquish the shame that feeds into pain; it's time to find purpose, and it's most definitely time to reclaim the power within us every single day. Can you feel it?

The power behind your thoughts impacts your whole body, and all of this power sits with you! How great is that?

The first foundation of Integrated Healing is understanding and accepting the six rules you need to break to start healing so you have realistic expectations to begin your journey.

Secondly, I will outline the daily pillars, practices, and perspectives you'll focus on and prioritise each day from the moment you open your eyes to the world in the morning and as you move through your day, interacting with people (or not) and managing the emotions, stress, and toxicity that can arise. You might need a pen to write down some notes about these practical changes.

Thirdly, I will summarise the principles to address and maintain to loosen the shackles of chronic pain. If you keep these principles at the forefront of your mind, healing will naturally follow.

Firstly, let's look at the six rules you need to break to start healing.

SIX RULES YOU NEED TO BREAK TO START HEALING

1. There is a one-size-fits-all approach to healing.

No, there isn't! Despite what you may have been told or

conditioned to think, there is no one-size-fits-all approach to healing. There is no benchmark to work towards in any healing or recovery. There is only an individual path of learning what works specifically for you, which may not work for me, and that's okay. We're all uniquely individual and will respond to different treatments based on numerous contributing factors, including genetic, mental, emotional, and physical make-up. Additional factors, such as psychosocial, environmental, cultural, religious, and personal preferences, may influence this even further. Only you know what's best and what aligns with your key values, so there's no need to compare your journey to anyone else's. Comparing yourself only limits you and keeps you small. It doesn't enable you to reclaim your power.

2. Healing is linear.

No, it's not! When healing, there isn't a single trajectory you follow. Practitioners can try to tell you what to expect, but there's often a number of different variables that can alter this path. There isn't one single framework to heal from chronic pain, and there's no step-by-step process that provides you with a 100 percent success rate. Otherwise, I wouldn't be sitting here writing this book, and we wouldn't need so many different self-help books. Healing isn't simply meditating, breathing, and sitting on a mountain top. At times, I wish it were that easy.

The truth is, we humans are complex beings. Chronic pain is also complex, and healing is about uncovering all the things that have manifested within our body and kept us from not moving forward mentally, emotionally, and physically. Sometimes, it can feel like you're taking one slow step at a time; other times, you may feel like you've deviated sideways, and other times you may feel like you've gone backwards. This is all okay and is most definitely part of the experience.

3. Life is only about healing.

No, it's not! Sometimes, while doing all this work and finally starting to feel better, we can become fixated (above all else) on healing, fixing, and doing. We can become so trapped in the mindset of constantly needing to improve that we forget that life is about living. You may have heard that we're human beings, not human doings. Being encompasses a different energy and frequency, so shifting our mindset to do more of what we love is crucial.

When we have autoimmunity and pain, we're often trapped in a cycle of constantly fixing, consumed with too many specialist doctors, too much prodding, and too much analysing. This causes us to lead from the analytical ego mind as opposed to feeling from the heart space and undertaking the things that light our fire and soul's purpose. Too much time in the analytical ego mind neglects the soul aspects that create who we are.

Our purpose in life isn't to heal; our purpose is to live.

We've forgotten that the true essence and purpose of life is to fully experience all aspects of life instead of being so focused on one element of it – in this case, pain.

Eliminating pain isn't your purpose; living a life full of love, freedom, joy, and a variety of experiences is. Reducing the pain will give you more freedom and choice, but you must ensure that you lead with what you want to bring into and embody in your life every day. This will keep you motivated and inspired instead of focusing on the negativity of pain, which can keep you at a standstill.

4. Life is a race.

No, it's not! Life isn't a race; neither is healing. Living with autoimmunity, a heightened nervous system, fatigue issues, or multiple conditions while trying to juggle the everyday requirements of life can create a self-perpetuating cycle. Trying to do too much of anything, even too much of a good thing, can be detrimental and impact our physical and energetic body, causing even more fatigue and even more symptoms to surface.

Do the initial reflection work and understand where your starting point is, what your stress triggers are, what makes you feel good, and what causes your body to feel not so good, and create a plan thereafter. Understand that this, too, can change as you improve, heal, and evolve. Take the time to reflect often and congratulate yourself on your achievements. Learn to be your biggest cheerleader.

Also, learn to let go of all expectations. This doesn't mean not having goals, but expectations about ourselves and our body can be restrictive. They can keep us trapped in how we think and behave, and we become so focused on achieving a certain end goal that we fail to listen to our body's cues, to pivot, adapt, and even rest when required. Essentially, we might not realise what our body needs in the long term.

Learning how to be present with what your body requires from you daily will be life-changing for you in the long term.

Learning how to be fluid and flexible in your mindset and behaviour is crucial for success.

Also, we need to remember that good things take time. Just like a seed needs time to sprout and grow, we're no different. Books take time to write; relationships take time to develop, and healing takes time too. But many people are in a rush to remove their trauma, to remove those deeply invasive roots and discard them, thinking that something new and amazing will grow in its place within a day or two.

Everything takes time: planting, watering, tending, nourishing, waiting for enough nutrients for the seeds to sprout and emerge. Our body can do so much if given enough time and support. We need to learn to trust the flow of life, trust the flow of the lessons.

We need to continue to focus on our vision and keep that intention at the forefront of each of our days.

5. Letting go (detoxing) is easy.

No, it certainly is not! As a generation Xer, I remember the numerous detox remedies my mum and her girlfriends would undertake, consuming gallons of fresh juices and drinking a concoction of naturopathic herbs to eliminate toxins and detoxify the body.

In today's era, my perception of detoxing is vastly different from the idea of a quick and easy five-day juice fast. If only it were that easy! For me, detoxing involves looking at the whole body, that is, how our thoughts, behaviours, emotions, and even the chemicals within our environment can create a toxic load and imprint within the body on a cellular, subconscious, physical, mental, and emotional level. For many of us, this accumulation of toxins contributes heavily towards our pain, our fatigue, and the discomfort within ourselves and our body. Most of us carry all this baggage and weight, plus expectations, stories, and limiting beliefs, within our body. On top of this is the generational trauma from our parents and ancestors that, too, has formed who we are and our belief systems. We harbour all of this internally like a huge weight on our back, yet wonder why we're struggling under the weight of it all.

The load can be heavy and arduous, but because we've carried it for so long, it has become extremely familiar. Letting go of anything that has formed who we are today can be difficult because it challenges everything we've learnt to date, including who we are. Detoxing and letting go can create discomfort within the body. As the toxins surface, it can bring a physical release, but because there's a process of unlearning, it can also create an emotional response that can comprise loss, grief, and sadness. All of this can feel unfamiliar, scary, and uncomfortable, and it can cause us to feel unsafe.

Like a juice detox, letting go can feel awful and hard as it passes through our body. Once it has cleared, it energetically provides room to focus on new beginnings. The energy we once exerted to carry the oppressive load of life is now free to be directed to things that create joy.

At times, the journey can feel tedious. It can challenge you mentally, physically, and emotionally. However, it will also enable you to go through the most monumental growth and evolution to discover and witness your power and strength as a human being and to emerge from what feels dark and heavy into something beautiful. That beauty is rediscovering *you*.

> "We must let go of the life we have planned, so as to accept the one that is waiting for us."
> **– Joseph Campbell**

6. Compare yourself to the old days.

No, don't look back! Looking back on the fond memories is beautiful. My gorgeous son is extremely nostalgic and loves to remember and reflect on memories and life experiences. This helps him to cherish and appreciate his life. This isn't what I'm referring to but rather how one of the biggest challenges to embracing change is accepting who we are today (with the limitations or restrictions that we may have) versus the person we used to be and desiring to be that again.

We often miss old aspects of ourselves because they enable us to live the life we currently desire, so we reminisce and reflect, pondering how we can return to this old life and existence. It causes us to continually compare our current self to old versions of ourselves, preventing us from moving forward and accepting **who we are right now at this point in time.**

The other side to this is that many people forget who they are because their limited energy and resources are being directed solely at treating the pain as though it has always been there. They've simply forgotten because their life has been taken over by their symptoms, pain, and trauma, and they're forced to attend countless medical appointments. They've been trying to alleviate symptoms in this perpetual mode of doing that's on a sliding scale downwards. There's an imbalance, and we need to start to shift the focus away from the pain and first remember the things we love to do and bring them back into our lives again, even on a small scale, so they create joy (because shifting our focus creates good feelings within us and, in turn, shifts the pain).

You're still the same person you were. Yes, at this point in time, you have some limitations and restrictions because of what's occurring within your physical body, but you can't allow these limitations to consume you. Fundamentally, you, at your core, are the same person you were before you were diagnosed or before your condition emerged. You still have the same attributes, the same personality, and we just need to bring more of these into focus.

You are not your pain; you are not your trauma; you are not your symptoms; you are not your experiences. You are so much more!

THE FOUR PILLARS OF DISRUPTING PAIN

Within this section, I will provide you with a framework of what I believe works best to start to break through the strongholds of chronic pain. I will rely on an integrated approach, focusing on tools that help you create change within your mind, body (emotional and physical), and soul.

For those of us who experience chronic pain and chronic symptoms, too much of our lives are directed towards managing what's occurring within our body. We've lost and forgotten many parts of ourselves, but it's time for us to retrieve them. We want to start to shift this now because, to date, what you've been doing hasn't been working, or you desire so much more for yourself and your life

It will require you to commit yourself by investing the time every day to do the inner work to get to know who you are without any of the limitations and labels of conditions.

I want you to fundamentally know who you are, without all the social conditioning, labels, and expectations.

From a mindset perspective, this will require you to tune into some of your subconscious beliefs and thought processes surrounding your diagnosis, condition, and behaviours.

It's time to get real and look at exactly how we release, reduce, and rebuild certain elements in our lives. Getting to know yourself can be hard; it can be challenging; it can cause a myriad of emotions to surface. You may also start to experience resistance and self-doubt, especially when things become uncomfortable. The brain works in fun ways to try to keep us safe and to maintain our status quo. When we feel challenged or feel discomfort, it can often cause us to feel unsafe, and, because of this, we retreat or flee, but the truth is that you are safe within your body and within this life, so don't give up. Please persevere and be gentle and kind with yourself and to yourself.

Also, please remember the six rules you need to break to start healing. These will be crucial for you as a reminder not to fall back into the old way of thinking, especially when you feel that you're not making the gains you desire. Things take time, and this is especially the case when healing a body that has endured chronic conditions for so long.

The Four Pillars

Understanding and releasing emotions: We'll look at it from a psychosomatic perspective, how you store pain, stress and emotions within your body, and how they can be released.

Rebuilding your nervous system: We will also look at ways to help rebuild your nervous system while rebuilding strength in your whole body, that is, within your mind and body.

Reducing toxic load: From a physical perspective, we will look at how you can reduce your daily toxic load to reduce the stresses that affect your physical body.

Creating a relationship with yourself: Last but not least, I will guide you on how to create a relationship with yourself because, ultimately, how you view yourself and how you treat yourself will underpin every decision you make, which impacts your whole body.

Pillar One – Understanding and Releasing Emotions

In previous sections, we highlighted the physical and psychological impact of living with chronic illness, chronic symptoms, and chronic pain. We also explored how our upbringing heavily influences our belief system, which, in turn, may influence how we perceive and view ourselves. Emotions are linked to our mental state (both our mind and thoughts) and involve conscious and subconscious processes that combine to form the experience of an emotion. How we view ourselves can elicit a huge emotional response. How we've been treated, our experiences, our upbringing, parental and societal expectations, cultural influences, and even our hopes and dreams all have an impact on our mental health, and this, in turn, impacts our emotions.

Throughout the process of living with chronic illness and chronic pain, it's likely you have experienced feelings of frustration, anger, sadness, disappointment, and so on. At times, you may not have had the opportunity to express these emotions and, even worse, may not have been validated and heard by those around you. Because of your experience, a further subsection of emotions may have emerged. If we look at emotions as energy within motion (e-motion), we can start to understand how certain emotions, when not processed and when not expressed, can then become stored within our body. The heavier emotions like fear, guilt, and shame carry a dense frequency. Carrying these for a long time can have a huge impact on us mentally, emotionally, and physically. The accumulative impact of this is stored within us, causing even more trauma to the body.

In this section, we will start to explore your relationship with emotions.

Firstly, you need to identify your most prominent emotions and then understand what programs are attached to them. Having the ability to delve into why you think and behave the way you do enables you to be more empowered. Observing your behaviour allows you to step away from it and become more objective and compassionate about your past and any insecurities that may arise. This awareness will help you acknowledge and accept how these powerful emotions have seemingly taken over your life, and gradually you can start to shift the frequency within your body to attract higher frequencies.

Remember, there are no right or wrong answers, but taking the time to understand who you are and why provides powerful insight into why you think, feel, and behave in certain ways.

During your childhood and upbringing, were you…

Taught that some emotions were bad to express while others weren't? What emotions were considered good and what emotions were considered bad?

Told off, punished, or made to feel bad for expressing yourself or emotions? If yes, which emotions were you told off for and how did this make you feel?

Taught that in order to be loved and accepted by either your friends, family, parents, or teachers, you needed to behave a certain way? What was this way?

Taught that emotions are gender specific? For example, boys shouldn't cry. If boys cry, it means they are weak. What gender specific rules about emotions were you taught?

Allowed to express emotions in a healthy way? In what ways were you encouraged to express your emotions, and are there certain emotions you feel more comfortable expressing over others? What are these?

Taught that, in order to be good or approved of, you or your body needed to behave or look a certain way? Where did you learn this from and what were you taught that your body needed to look like in order to be approved of? Is this still the case today, or has this changed and evolved?

Exploring the Emotions Attached to Your Diagnosis

A diagnosis can often be liberating and comforting, providing you with an explanation for why you may be experiencing symptoms and what might be occurring within your body. However, along with a diagnosis, a myriad of different emotions can appear.

Here is a list of primary emotions. I'd like you to circle the emotions you've felt since your diagnosis or since your health concerns emerged.

Anger	Fear	Helplessness
Peace	Courage	Shame
Sadness	Frustration	Pride
Hope	Gratitude	Inspiration
Resentment	Guilt	Motivation
Acceptance	Loneliness	

1. Can you see a pattern with the emotions that you listed?
2. At what frequency are the emotions that you feel or have experienced? Beside each circled emotion, write either 1 (rarely), 2 (sometimes), or 3 (often).

Understanding Your Emotions Questionnaire

When answering the following questions, please look at the previously listed emotions (where applicable) and list which emotions relate to the question, plus any further information.

Since your diagnosis, how have you felt about your body, and what emotion does this elicit?

....

....

....

....

....

....

....

....

....

....

....

....

....

Do you think this belief and emotion about your body stems from yourself or someone else?

How have other people made you feel about what is happening with your body?

How have you felt supported? If you haven't felt supported, how has this made you feel?

At any point, have you been made to feel bad about your condition? What emotions did this make you feel?

At any point, have you been made to blame? How has this made you feel?

There Is No Need to Fear Fear!

For so much of our lives, we're told to fear the big scary things. We're told to protect ourselves from all the big bads. We're told to fear the unknown, fear autoimmunity, fear life, but fear is actually an emotional response to an underlying emotion. It can be extremely insightful if you delve into what underlies your fear.

These are some of the fears that emerged for me over the years:

- Fear attached to what is happening within my body.
- Fear of how I will manage a life of uncertainty.
- Fear of the unknown.
- Fear of the unseen cost of living with a chronic condition.
- Fear attached to possibly never living a 'normal' life again.
- Fear of judgement from those around me, especially my family and friends.
- Fear of not being seen or heard by practitioners, specialists, within the community, and by loved ones.
- Fear of what my life will become.

So much fear, yet the fear masked the emotions of helplessness, powerlessness, shame, resentment, and unworthiness. Sound familiar?

When I decided to explore and delve beneath the fear, I realised all these emotions related to my need to feel safe and secure. As humans, feeling safe and secure is a primal need. If we don't feel safe and secure, whether within our body or our immediate environment, it creates a feeling of panic within the body. It also generates a physiological response where we want to escape the situation, which causes the fear (think running away from the bear trying to attack us), but much of the fear is aligned with our own thoughts.

Fear isn't always bad, as self-protection can save us in certain situations, but if we allow it to dictate our lives, it keeps us feeling small and living in fear. Exploring what it is that doesn't allow us to feel safe is key, and this is often linked to our programming.

Once we have the awareness, we can start to break down and dismantle some of the mindset limitations that keep us small.

Reflect and take the time to answer these questions honestly and openly. Understanding your fear is so crucial in enabling you to take control of this emotion.

What fears have you experienced since your diagnosis?

What fears do you have in relation to your body?

What fears do you have in relation to your life?

What fears do you have in relation to your own personal goals and dreams?

What do you think underlies all these fears? For example, *Not being able to participate in the things that I love makes me feel isolated and disconnected, and this triggers because I feel unwanted and unloved.*

Does your condition make you feel less worthy, less important, less active within the community? Why do you believe this is?

Do you feel less worthy because you cannot achieve the outcomes you desire? How does this make you feel, and where does this emotion sit within your body?

....
....
....
....
....
....
....
....
....
....
....
....
....
....
....
....
....
....
....

Do you feel judged because of what is happening within your body? How does this make you feel, and where does this emotion sit within your body?

Do you believe you have had to sacrifice parts of yourself and your life? When you think about this, how does it make you feel? Where does that emotion sit within your body?

When you think of your future, what is the primary narrative, and what emotions arise?

The Origins of Our Programming

The programs we have, or the stories we tell ourselves, are often a by-product of our environment and upbringing. Raising awareness of the programs within and around us is another imperative step to creating an understanding of – and compassion around – how we react to many situations, why we react the way we do, and why we behave in certain ways. For example, I've spent many years unknowingly partaking in activities and behaviours that went against my personal boundaries to please others so I would feel loved and accepted. My inner child believed that this was what was required in order to feel worthy. My adult self soon learnt that this programming was my default and I no longer needed to engage in activities that went against my personal boundaries or values in order to please someone else.

Examples of the programming around us are our parents' expectations of how they believe we need to be or act, our friends' belief systems that we unconsciously absorb, or even our educational and governmental systems and structures. These programs may also be imposed by our doctors' or practitioners' beliefs and expectations, or even our own personal beliefs and expectations of how we need to be, which influence how we need to behave and sometimes perform. These expectations become programmed into us, and the corresponding emotional response and pressure can cause us to behave in a certain way, limiting us from moving forward.

Different types of programs I've identified and had to break are:

- I need to be healthy to contribute to society.
- I am a failure because my body doesn't adhere to society's expectations of what is healthy.
- I am a burden on the system because I need support.
- I am invisible because I have an invisible illness.
- I am less than someone who doesn't have an invisible illness.
- I am not worthy because I don't work, or I don't work as much as someone else. I must be a burden because I need to physically, financially, and emotionally rely on someone else.
- Something must be wrong with me because I don't seem to have it all together.
- I am weak because I need guidance and support.
- If I am not working, then I am not successful, so I must work.
- I am broken because my mind and body function differently from the 'norm'.
- To be successful, I need to work.
- My worth is based upon my financial contributions; therefore, if I am not bringing sufficient income, I must not be worthy.

Now, take the time to reflect if any additional programs have surfaced for you.

Reprogramming Your Existing Belief System

What is the biggest program you have encountered since being diagnosed?

How long have you been carrying this thought process?

How has this influenced your perception of who you are today?

When you delve deeper, is this your belief or someone's who is external to you, for example, your parents or a practitioner?

What new empowering belief statement can you replace with this?

Positive Mindset Equals New Neural Pathways and Positive Behavioural Patterns

A further way to delve into the limitations you associate with your health or pain is to explore how your symptoms may have triggered certain related emotions. If we're aware of this, we can start to break the negative thought pattern or loop and replace it with a more positive thought or action.

Some examples you might say to yourself:

- My condition seems to have worsened, and because of this I have fears over my future.
- Fatigue and tiredness have caused me to decline social events and to shut off from the external world, and because of this I feel lonely and controlled by what is happening within my body.
- Lack of understanding about my condition means that I don't have support, and because of this I feel unheard and isolated.
- Active and high achieving people seem to trigger me because they're a constant reminder that I can't achieve the things I want, and because of this I feel ashamed, embarrassed, and often resentful.
- Brain fog means that it's hard to concentrate or mentally and cognitively achieve what I used to, and because of this I feel angry.
- Sound and light sensitivity mean that I need to be extra diligent about where I go out, and because of this I feel frustrated.

Let's start to reframe this mindset to be more empowered when we think about our symptoms.

> **Old Mindset:** My condition seems to worsen, and because of this I have fears over my future.
>
> **New Mindset:** Each and every day, I am becoming more and more aware of my body and her symptoms. My body communicates through the show of symptoms, creating an opportunity for me to ask her what she needs from me to support her. Although the fear is real, I choose not to sit within the frequency of fear, and I shift this by focusing on my body's capabilities as opposed to its inabilities. I listen to my body and support her accordingly. I am grateful for what I can achieve while learning to be compassionate to myself for things I feel I can't achieve, knowing that this time is not permanent.

> **Old Mindset:** Fatigue and tiredness have caused me to decline social events and to shut off from the external world, and because of this I feel lonely.

New Mindset: Although I'm tired, I choose to honour my body's needs. Although I feel lonely and isolated, I choose not to isolate myself and close myself off from others. When my energy is restored, I will connect with the ones I love and know they're there to support and love me without judgement, at any given point. I do not need to isolate myself from others, create stories, or judge myself for this.

Old Mindset: Sound and light sensitivity mean that I need to be extra diligent about where I go out, and because of this I feel frustrated.

New Mindset: As sound and light affect me, I make an empowered choice not to expose myself to environments that do not serve me. I also acknowledge that my increased sound and light sensitivity may mean that my nervous system needs a little bit more support. I do not need to be on guard or explain myself to others. I will continue to expose myself to the environments that enable my body to thrive.

We can become more objective if we learn to look for the societal structures and expectations that contribute to some of these negative emotions.

Expectations such as:
- I am only worthy if I work Monday to Friday, nine to five.
- I need to be equal in financial and energetic contributions within my household and relationship.
- I am not a fit mum if I don't have it 'all together' – household, cooking, school activities, 'perfect' kids.
- I am not a fit father if I don't have it 'all together' – being the provider and a good role model.
- I am disabled because I have an invisible illness.

What stigmas (if any) have arisen with your diagnosis, and what emotions has this produced? For example for some, alongside the diagnosis can come shame and guilt. If shame produces guilt within you, take the opportunity to look at where this is coming from and if it's yours or a projection from others. For example, *I feel guilty for not being able to work.*

It's Time to Write a List

Now take the time to list all the beliefs, expectations, and emotions you no longer want to hold onto.

Tips…
- ~ Relinquish the guilt around what you believe you must achieve to please those around you.

- ~ Relinquish the guilt around what you believe you must achieve to be approved by society.
- ~ Relinquish the guilt around what you believe you need to achieve in order to be successful.
- ~ Relinquish the guilt around how you believe you need to be seen in order to be 'healing' or 'healed'.

Although doing the inner work and delving in deep to understand why you are the person you are today can be hard, it's also unbelievably empowering and insightful. I hope doing these exercises has given you insights to understand how and why you are the person you are today. Start to take charge and see where you can begin to let go of all the existing programs, structures, other people's beliefs and expectations, and associated stigmas that do not serve you. See how much this frees you up mentally, emotionally, and energetically and now gives you the opportunity to focus on the things that light you up.

Pillar Two – Rebuilding Your Nervous System

When we start to understand how we've been raised and how this, in turn, impacts our programming, down to the way we receive information, how we behave, and how we react, we can also start to understand why certain things impact our body. For example, some people will naturally react more to stress than others. For those with chronic illness and chronic pain, it appears that the experience of prolonged suffering can cause stress on the body, which, in turn, confuses the central nervous system. Thus, our central nervous system can begin to misinterpret a vast array of stimuli as painful and threatening, impacting how we react, whether consciously or subconsciously. This creates an immense amount of pressure on our central nervous system. Often, because of this, undertaking small tasks can create a huge physiological demand on our body. Finding ways to manage our symptoms and help our nervous system regulate and become stable is crucial to healing the whole body.

Your Body Needs to Feel Safe

For your body to start regulating itself, it needs to feel safe. It must feel that it isn't running away from things that may harm her. For those with chronic symptoms, it can be tough to reconcile this because pain can cause you to feel like you are being harmed. In previous sections, we've alluded to the fact that it doesn't matter if it's a real threat or a perceived threat we're exposed to. Our body cannot differentiate between the two of them and will believe it is real regardless. This is why it is our job to teach and guide our brain and our body to stop being alarmed.

I will now tell you something radical that most other practitioners will never ever tell you.

You need to stop fighting. You need to stop fighting your pain. You need to stop fighting your thoughts. You need to stop fighting yourself.

Now, let me clarify.

I do not mean to give up on yourself. I mean to stop being at war with yourself, to stop the polarity with yourself, to stop the internal conflict, to stop the judgement, to stop thinking that you need to fight your symptoms, your circumstances and your life.

I need you to put down your sword.

I need you to stop fighting.

Stop fighting yourself. Stop fighting your thoughts. Stop fighting against your emotions. Stop fighting against your diagnosis. Stop fighting against your condition. Stop fighting against your expectations. Stop fighting against others' expectations of you.

Fighting means your body will remain on high alert and sensitive to perceived threats. It will continue to fall into patterns of fight and flight. When your body doesn't need to be on guard, it can direct its energy to managing the symptoms and reducing the pain without continuing this perpetual cycle of pain and inflammation. In turn, you will be able to focus your energy on helping your body to know that she is safe, not needing to be so hypervigilant to external stimuli and creating new behaviours to strengthen and support your body.

Why Do We Not Feel Safe?

As a child and a teenager, I would experience moments of panic, moments that often overwhelmed me and were fear-driven. Often, I would fear dying. At the time, I didn't know they were panic attacks and that these moments of panic were underlying something bigger.

Sometimes, even today, I get this awful feeling out of nowhere that tells me I'm not safe. It's usually in the middle of the night.

An irrational thought will creep in and tell me that I need to be fearful, that I need to be on guard, that something bad might be about to happen.

Let me also clarify that these aren't instinctual gut feelings that alert me to needing to be on guard. I'm usually tucked up in bed, and my thoughts and the noise in my head cause me to spiral to places that make me feel unsafe and want to hide away from the world. So much of the anxiety and nervousness within our body relate to fears over our life, and sometimes our mind takes us to places that don't serve us.

I hope this section allows you to implement some tools that help ease some of the nervousness, some of the anxiety, and some of the fear you have around what's happening with your body.

Much of our fear, anxiety, and feelings of not being enough stem from our childhood, from times and experiences where we didn't feel enough. When we don't feel safe, we often default to these experiences, which remind us that we need to protect ourselves, that we need to be on guard.

Neuroplasticity allows us to change these fear-based thoughts into what many of us like to call divine truths. Divine truths are truths that are infinite in wisdom and power. They don't limit us; they only propel us forward in remembering our body's potent ability to heal. They aren't ego-driven; they don't cause us to seek an unfilled need because divine truths know that we're already filled with love and everything we'll ever need. We just need to tune into this button, turn the switch on, and then remind ourselves of this every single day.

For this pillar, we'll focus on implementing tools that help guide our nervous system in not needing to be on guard and attacking itself and its body. It's not about overhauling your life and overwhelming your system even more; it's about giving you practical strategies to gently restore ease to your life and rebalance your nervous system so it doesn't feel that it needs to fight and attack everyone and everything.

Without a doubt, change can cause us to feel unsafe when we default to old beliefs and patterns that propel us out of our comfort zone. Often, our inner child adamantly believes they'll cause us harm – but they won't.

Before we start, we need to be intentional with our approach. So often, we look at the big picture – of being free of pain, free of fatigue, free of the oppressiveness, free of anxiety, or whatever else it may be. We then become so overwhelmed at the enormity of what it takes to get to this ideal that we retreat inwards and do nothing.

To create change, we must plant small seeds, continue to water them, and enable them to grow into bigger things.

Today, I commit to discovering who I am, to making the effort to learn the things I love, to stop the self-hatred, to stop being so hard on myself.

Instead, I commit to planting small seeds that include:
- Leading with love and compassion for myself.
- To stop beating myself up.
- To stop falling into victim mode.
- To implement practices that remind my body that she is

loved and that she is safe, and when she feels like she isn't, to acknowledge this and reframe my mind.
- To prioritise myself and my needs.
- To rest when I need to.
- To ask for help and support.
- To not isolate myself.
- To know that I have the strength and courage to create change.

Why Rest Is So Important

Bodies that have been in high stress, experienced long-term chronic pain, and been in fight and flight have exceptionally heightened nervous systems. This means that the smallest amount of perceived stress, including noise, people, bright lights, foods such as caffeine, and anything the body thinks is a stress, can cause a response within. Anything rushed can cause our body to feel under duress.

As it has tried to fight off pain and fatigue, your body has been in a state of hypervigilance and fight-or-flight, so if you're wondering why you're so tired, this is why. Your body needs deep rest, and for a lot longer than you might expect. Gentleness and slowness are crucial to help restore your nervous system, as are deep restorative rest and sleep.

Returning to the Body

Being in fight and flight also means there's a level of disassociation with what's occurring within our body. As long-term pain sufferers, we do this as a means of escape, but there comes a point where we can no longer escape. Because of this, we can disconnect and separate ourselves from the feelings within the body.

The goal is to become embodied, that is, return to the body and acknowledge what it needs to do to stay alive. You can also practise active listening to what your body needs, that is, tuning in and listening to its cues, the tension that may reside, the stress that's sitting within your face and jaw, and the stagnant emotions that have been suppressed and are asking to be acknowledged and seen. All of this is integral to developing a relationship with and returning to yourself. Just like any relationship, it takes time. It cannot be pushed or forced.

Start Your Day with Slowness

There are several steps you can take to start your day with slowness and support your nervous system. As you read this, the list isn't designed to overwhelm you but to provide you with options. Creating a new habit can be hard, and often our brain will tell us that it's not working, not worth it, or too hard. Identify when this arises and try to simply incorporate one or two suggestions to start off with and build up slowly and gently with no pressure:

- Awaken 20 minutes prior to needing to start your day to avoid the need to rush.
- Start your day with 5 minutes of gentle slow breathing to help awaken your body.
- Practise 5 minutes of gratitude at the start of the day.

- Consume something nourishing to help your hormones and support your adrenals.
- Incorporate gentle movements, like Pilates or yoga, to encourage your body to move.
- *Repeat* each day.

To support your efforts, you should also avoid anything that causes your body to feel stressed.

Reduce Stress on the Nervous System

When your body is too busy fighting stressors, it's extremely hard for you to introduce new behaviours and new patterns. Trying to add something on top, even the simplest of new behaviours, can overwhelm the mind and body. This is why creating new behaviours can be challenging – because not only is your body fighting pain and symptoms and imbalances, introducing something new can cause your brain and body to feel unsafe and, in turn, cause a physical reaction within the body.

There was a time not so long ago when I was deep in the throes of fibro symptoms and chronic pain and my nervous system was so dysregulated, thanks to decades of fighting and surviving, that I couldn't stand going to the shops with the people, the crowds, the bright lights, and so forth. One small trip could throw me for the rest of the afternoon, if not for a few days. Even sitting in a café with groups of people would overwhelm my system over time. However, as my nervous system has become more and more regulated, my body doesn't get as overwhelmed, but I know that when I'm tired, small things do still trigger it. My brain is often at full capacity, and the smallest of things can take me over the edge. This could be music blaring too loudly, or being in a small, confined space with numerous people talking, or even simply someone trying to converse with me. Regardless of what it is, my body is letting me know that it's too much and too much stress is being placed on me all at once. Remember – our body is clever like that. She will always let us know if something is too much, and instead of shutting her down and dismissing her, listen and acknowledge what's being communicated.

Regulating your nervous system is a pivotal aspect of helping reduce your symptoms, as well as reprogramming and addressing deep-seated subconscious thoughts and behaviours that are causing you to either remain in survival mode or default to inherent patterns of survival mode. It can be hard, and it can be exhausting, so please give yourself some grace instead of beating yourself up.

Expanding your body's ability to hold more is also important. It's a fine balance between honouring what your body needs, building resistance and agility, and not sitting in your limitations. This is such a pivotal part of not placing limitations or restrictions over your body.

How to Create a Safe Space for Yourself

I have spent hours and hours and hours within my home in order to heal and restore my body. Many people who are recovering from chronic illness, chronic fatigue, and chronic symptoms often need to spend many hours in deep rest and restoration to heal their body. Our body is our home, and our home houses our body, so, for us to feel safe, we must create a sanctuary within our homes. Creating a sanctuary and safe space within my home has been crucial, especially when I felt confined and limited. When we reside in an environment that allows us to feel safe, we let go and soften, which does wonders for our nervous system and our body's ability to feel safe.

Here are some tips for creating a safe space for yourself:

- Identify what feels good for your nervous system. What does this look like in relation to colours, sounds, textures, smells, music, plants, and so on?
- Create a mood board, get expressive and creative, add some of your favourite quotes or photos of memories that take you to a place that feels good deep within your soul.
- Add scents and smells. All oils and scents have a frequency attached to them and can lift our mood within a matter of seconds. They can also elicit beautiful memories and transport us to other places
- Add pictures of your favourite places. As you heal, you may feel like you're confined to your home. Visualising and looking at your favourite places, such as the beach, the outdoors, or different countries, can shift your brain patterns and change your mood.
- Add music. Music is extremely powerful in setting the scene and creating an environment to elicit powerful emotions within you. Leverage this.

Digital Detox

With the increase in social media and advancements in technology, many of us are on our devices from the moment we wake to when we go to bed. For many of us who are restricted physically, social media can provide a way to connect and feel validated by people who are experiencing similar ailments and symptoms. It can, however, create unhealthy addictions and cause us to be bombarded with useless information that doesn't allow our brain, let alone our mind, body, and spirit, the opportunity for quietness and stillness. It also doesn't provide the type of real human connection that's crucial for us.

Take the opportunity to see where you're relying unhealthily on social media and how you can replace this with real ways to connect to humans. This, too, will give you more energy to focus on the things that are important to you. Your nervous system will also thank you. Personally, the biggest tip I found to assist my nervous system was to turn off all notifications on my phone. It gave me the power to be in control of when I accessed information and how much information I took in at any given time. Remember, we hold the power. Don't let technology or social media take it away from us.

Connection

Pain can restrict us from connecting with the outer world and others to form deep, loving connection. Heartache can also cause us to close ourselves off from forming deep relationships and connections due to fear of being hurt. In addition to this, many of us are becoming disconnected from the physical world we live in due to our busy lives, technological advancements, social media, and so on. For our health and wellbeing, it's crucial that we reconnect.

1. Connect within the world we live in, the true world, that of mother nature.
Elements like grounding, moving, or exercising allow us to get outside and view Mother Nature in her glory.

2. Connect with each other.
Heartfelt relationships are key to nurturing and sustaining each and every one of us and are known to positively elicit powerful hormones and emotions that are crucial for our wellbeing. Disconnecting from technology and talking and connecting with others is necessary to develop meaningful relationships.

3. Connect with ourselves.
Disconnecting from technology and allowing space within our lives enables us to connect with ourselves.

Do What Makes You Feel Good!

Make small changes that won't blow your energetic system or your nervous system but are amazing for the body, mind, and soul. For me, these were some life-changing actions I could easily implement, even when I had chronic, debilitating pain and all-consuming fatigue, all while managing kids and the expectations of life. Sometimes you need to reduce your expectations.

To make change manageable and create new habits over time, I decided to commit to one small task. Just one. Then I repeated this every day for a couple of weeks, adding another item based on my energy levels. It was an ongoing commitment to creating change and bettering myself.

Over the years, through this strategy, I've built up my tool bag of resources. No, I don't have the time to implement each tool every day, but I do use many of them frequently in my daily routine, so much so that they're now instinctual and I can use them without needing to force it. When I don't commit to using my tools, I find that I start to spiral and become disconnected from myself. When I do use them, they help me become embodied, change my perspective, and focus on the good, positive things I can control.

The amazing thing – all of the following recommendations are free. They don't cost a thing to implement. Over time, feel free to expand this list and create your own tool bag of resources.

- ~ 5 minutes of gratitude
- ~ 5 minutes of breathing and meditation
- ~ 5 minutes of somatic movement
- ~ 5 minutes of deep connection with a partner or friend
- ~ 5 minutes of dry brushing
- ~ 5 minutes of self-massage
- ~ 5 minutes of affirmations
- ~ 5 minutes of grounding
- ~ 5 minutes of intentions

- 5 minutes of dancing
- 5 minutes of creativity
- 5 minutes of sunshine
- 5 minutes of visualisation
- 5 minutes of journalling
- 5 minutes of appreciation
- 5 minutes of hugging

Starting the Day Empowered

Simple everyday practices can be small but powerful. The intent is to create a routine that isn't arduous and overwhelming but one you can maintain.

Set an alarm for 15–20 minutes prior to you needing to get up. I wake, express gratitude for the day, and examine how my body is feeling. Sometimes she feels good; sometimes she feels heavy; sometimes she feels foggy, and sometimes I'm already checking my to-do list in my mind and feeling extremely anxious about it all. Sometimes negativity creeps in. Before I get too carried away, I gently go from a rested state and connect with my body to see what support I need and how I can achieve it with purpose and intent, without rushing.

Somatic Practice

Somatic practices are a powerful way of connecting back to your body, through mindfulness, gentle breathing, and movement. It also helps us to explore what emotions could be surfacing within the body and help to release them in a gentle manner, without triggering too much of a physical response. Somatic practices have been crucial in assisting with the regulation of my central nervous system.

A powerful morning practice that you could incorporate into your everyday routine is to connect to your body and acknowledge her. Take in five deep breaths. Draw the breath from your nose through your heart and into your belly. Then slowly release. Repeat this but also do this with intention, focusing on gratitude for your breath. Also focus on gratitude for the air you breathe.

Now focus on how your body feels. Is it sore? Is it achy? Does it feel restored after a good night's sleep? Listen intently with no need to question or judge whatever comes up.

If you feel the desire to go a little deeper, you can also be curious and start to ask

If there are any emotions attached to how your body feels. For example, if you've had a bad night's sleep, have aches and pains, and are feeling tired and cranky, does this bring up any additional emotions, for example, frustration and anger? If it doesn't, fine. If it does, can you sit with this without any judgement? Can you take the time to breathe into this and identify where it's sitting within your body? Can you identify any stories that you've attached to these feelings? Can you just sit with this for a mere moment and acknowledge it? When the time feels right, can you then feel into this emotion, hold on to it, then breathe deeply into your body and release it out through your mouth? This technique is powerful in honouring any emotions that surface or are triggered at any point and acknowledging them with kindness and compassion, instead of allowing frustration, anger, and annoyance to take the lead. Having the ability to recognise and label your emotions is one thing, but having the power to process and release them is another!

Toxic Positivity and Gratitude

While living a life of gratitude can help reframe your mindset, and law of attraction tells us that we think and believe becomes us, we also need to make sure we're not simply denying the expression of emotion or ignoring how we really feel, as this ends up being avoidance and can cause emotions to build up within the body. The trick is to simply honour any emotions that surface, while holding gratitude for your life experiences and where you are today.

Be aware of how much energy you're exerting on unnecessary thoughts and worries. See if you can shift and channel this into areas of your life that will benefit you. Your energy is limited, so you need to preserve it while building back the reserves, as opposed to worrying about all the external aspects of the world, how people may respond, or their reactions (think your sister, brother, parents, family, friends, and even your co-workers). Their worries, opinions, and thoughts aren't for you to take on at all. This is their own experience. Let that shit go by being conscious of every time a thought occurs that causes negative feelings. See where it takes you and how you can take control. Become super concrete. Tap into the heart space more, and instead of trying to rationalise everything, feel into it.

Redirecting Your Energy

Living with chronic symptoms, pain, and cycles of extreme fatigue has meant that I've had to be super diligent with how I exert myself to ensure that when I'm depleted, I take the opportunity to listen to my body and to rest. This means that I've had to not only implement strong boundaries with others but also boundaries with myself.

Doing this means identifying where you may be giving away your energy, for example, allowing limiting thoughts, staying in victim mode, serving too many people, engaging in conversations you aren't comfortable with, overcommitting yourself socially, exposing yourself to media and news channels that keep you trapped in fear, relying on social media – and the list goes on. When we give away our energy to such activities, we leave little for what our body requires in order to heal. Not only is preserving your energy crucial, but so is filling up and maintaining your energetic reserves so you can focus on the things you love and desire.

While we're on the topic, stop allowing people to think of you as needing to be fixed. You don't need fixing. You need time and space for deep rest and restoration, not their pity projected onto you. This also means implementing strong boundaries with yourself to not be in a perpetual state of healing, needing to get better, and over-burning your system. Remember, you are a powerful being. Things take time to heal, grow, and evolve. Be patient, and learn to say no more frequently!

Neuroplasticity

Living with chronic conditions, chronic pain, and chronic fatigue can not only diminish our ability to undertake simple everyday activities but also our joy for life. Instead of focusing on what you don't have, let's start to shift this narrative that's keeping you trapped, the one that kept me trapped for years.

Here are some beautiful prompts to reflect on:
- What are the things that make me feel good within myself?
- What are the things that bring me joy?
- How can I focus more on these aspects of my life?
- What am I grateful for?

We must make a conscious effort not to remain trapped and to instead call in and be open to receiving what our innermost being desires right now. For me, it meant changing the words I spoke about myself. It meant I had to stop hating on my body. It meant I had to stop projecting expectations on myself and stop comparing myself to others. It meant learning to listen to my body and connect back to her. It meant being in a relationship with her. It meant finding the positives in each and every day and moving out of the fear. Last but not least, it meant loving and accepting myself as I was, each and every day, with all my imperfections.

Repeat these statements every day, multiple times, and see if a shift begins.

- I am open to receiving.
- I love my body, and my body loves me.
- I love and accept myself.
- I am abundant.
- My cells know how to restore to their original state.
- I welcome in all that is aligned with my innermost being.
- Everything comes to me with ease and grace.

Surround yourself with good people. Surround yourself with people who believe in you, who encourage you, who are good for your mental health, your body, your nervous system, and your soul.

Detaching from Your Own Internal Dialogue

How many of us struggle with an internal dialogue each and every day? How many of us have to tell our ego to back off or to put him or her back in their place? I think it's all of us, and numerous times a day!

Your ego is the one who likes to tell you that you're not good enough. He or she also likes to attach themselves to stories, like, "You're not good enough because you're not pretty enough" and, "You don't earn enough money, you don't have enough followers or enough of a presence, so no one will want to hear what you have to say." The ego creates stories about us and likes to keep us on the merry-go-round, where we continue to rehash these stories. Many of us define ourselves by these stories and scenarios, allowing them to control us when, in actual fact, we have the power to detach from them. These stories are keeping us limited and from moving forward to create change – because we all know change can be scary, and scary can mean unsafe. They also keep us limited in our suffering and ability to partake in certain aspects of life.

We must take responsibility and be aware of the mental dialogue that emerges. We need to be aware of the stories and the attachments so we can identify when they are surfacing and take control and ownership of them. Having awareness of when our ego is leading us astray is a true gift.

Additional Questions

Here are some additional questions you can ask yourself to begin to reduce the negative impact on your nervous system:

- In what ways can I be kinder to myself?
- In what ways can I alleviate some of the stress in my life?
- Who can I call into my life to support me?
- In what ways can I nourish my body to support my healing?
- In what ways can I move my body to support it to heal?
- What do I love to do that will increase my good feeling hormones?
- In what timeframe can I start to implement this?

Get Out of Your Own Way

Many people with chronic pain, fatigue, and fibromyalgia are used to having to say no in order to preserve their energy. Saying no is so impactful, but we can become reliant on saying no, so much so that we remove ourselves from situations that serve us for fear of how they'll impact us energetically, or due to fear of experiencing a relapse. I often found myself saying no to social situations, to strengthening my body, to experiencing new experiences for fear of a relapse or fear of being bedridden for days or weeks on end. Saying no became my default.

Unfortunately, saying no can keep us trapped within limitations. It restricts social connection and can limit the opportunity to explore new avenues that enable growth. As humans, we're primed for social connection, so while there are times when saying no is important, you should also allow yourself to say yes! Identify how you need to support yourself in social situations – physically, emotionally, and energetically.

Give yourself permission to say no, but also give yourself permission to say yes. Rebuild the neural pathways that enable you to challenge yourself and to experience fun and joy! Surround yourself with people who are good for your mental health, your body, your nervous system, and your soul.

Pillar Three – Reducing Toxic Load

Traditionally, we've thought of stress as having too much pressure at work, too much pressure at home, financial pressures, and feeling pulled in different directions because we're trying to fulfil all of these. When I think of stress, I think of all the invisible stressors within us that have accumulated over our entire lives. These stressors are made up of your childhood experiences, the needs you didn't have met as a child, your thoughts, your mindset, the way you live your life, harboured emotions, decades of unresolved hurt and trauma, genetics, the modern way of living, increased exposure to chemicals, and not doing the things you simply love. All of these factors can create a huge energetic burden on the body that, in turn, can manifest physically and create further health imbalances and disease.

Whoa!

While that might be a lot to digest, it's the truth, which is why relying on one practitioner to 'fix' or heal you, or one modality to heal you, or one drug to treat everything will never provide you with the gains you desire. Because fundamentally, all of these things will continue brewing beneath the surface, knocking louder and louder until you acknowledge them.

Now, there are two ways you'll respond to this. You may be inclined to say, "Hell no" and instead decide to stick your head in the sand, avoid taking responsibility, and then wonder why you aren't getting the change you desire. This has been me.

I also know, on the other end of the spectrum, we can become all-consumed with trying to uncover all of our childhood traumas, defaulting to fix-it mode in an attempt to heal, yet we become so exhausted by the process. This, too, has been me.

The key is to gradually ease into this, to create awareness of who you are today and understand what and who has contributed to the person you are and, more importantly, the things that are causing pain and imbalances within your body. Secondary to this is to stop sitting within your own mental suffering, to harness your power, and to actively break some of the cycles that are contributing to your pain and symptoms. The premise of ALL of this is to identify ways that you can reclaim your power from the things that have been taking it away, for you to start to shift some of the toxic load from these items that have been weighing you down. Think about how much responsibility we carry from our everyday lives and then combine this with all the above. Relieving some of the heaviness and weight will free you up to redirect your energy and power into things that will benefit and serve you.

I urge you to explore this next section with curiosity and without judgement, judgement of yourself or judgement of others. If it does bring up certain emotions, experiences, and triggers, I would like you to pause and source people who can guide you through it.

Please also note that you don't need to overhaul your life in one go. Don't! Doing so will just trigger a response within the body or even shock your body too much, and you'll end up with a relapse or flare-up of symptoms. This journey is about learning to be kinder, gentler, and less angry with yourself.

True Acceptance of Who You Are Today

Healing autoimmunity, healing pain, healing chronic symptoms, and healing old wounds means learning how to accept all the 'not so worthy' or negative parts of ourselves. It means acknowledging and loving them, not trying to fix them or allowing them to define us but just acknowledging and accepting that they're fundamentally part of us. There's no right or wrong because all of these parts make up the sum of who we are.

Healing is learning to create loving bonds with each of these aspects of ourselves. Healing is developing relationships with all of these parts. How we perceive our body influences how we treat it, which subsequently communicates to our body whether or not we believe she is worthy to heal. The bonds we have with ourselves and our body form during childhood.

Now ask yourself the following questions.
- Have you been taught to lead with love or with judgement?
- How has this influenced how you treat your body?
- Have you encountered situations where others imposed judgement towards how you looked?
- How did this feel when you encountered such situations?

To understand why we carry some of these wounds, a beautiful and profound exercise is to sit and meet the younger version of ourselves, also known as our inner child. Our inner child carries a number of significant and often traumatic experiences that, in turn, influence who we are and why we behave in certain ways. These experiences become stuck within us and start to define who we are. Our inner child is also our subconscious version of ourselves. Therefore, a beautiful, empowering exercise is to go back to our childhood (from 0 to 18 years of age) and understand what experiences occurred for us that planted the seeds of disapproval or caused us to not feel worthy, loved, validated, shamed, and so on.

When we go back and meet our inner child, we can start to hold ourselves with compassion, understanding that, at times, we may have been hurt when instead we needed to be affirmed, loved, validated, and held with compassion by our parents, friends, or loved ones. As adults, we can attend to these unmet needs. We can also pull the old thoughts of not being enough, which don't serve us, and start to replace them with new thoughts filled with divine truths.

Exploring the Inner Child

Now it's time to explore your inner child. Before you begin the exercise, let me provide you with an example.

Example

Age: 6

Memory: Wearing a leotard and thinking I didn't fit in and my legs looked fat. I decided that my legs were disgusting and I wasn't worthy of being a ballerina.

How I felt: Embarrassed, ashamed, not worthy.

Thought and new belief I can create to replace this old memory and belief: My body is worthy. The size of my body and the size of my legs do not define me. I am beautiful, regardless. Every inch of my body is worthy and beautiful.

Age: 16

Memory: Living in a very white society and being exposed to subtle racism, even though I was Asian. Being dismissed for not being Asian and not being white.

How I felt: Uncomfortable within my own skin and like I needed to be whiter and more westernised in order to be accepted.

Thought and new belief I can create to replace this old memory and belief: My physical and cultural appearance do not define my worth. I am not defined by my colour or the way that I look. I love and accept my cultural heritage.

Exercise:

Now start to reflect and list some of your own personal experiences that occurred during your childhood and how you can start to shift some of the existing beliefs with new and correct truths.

Age:

Memory:

How I felt:

What I needed:

Thought and new belief I can create to replace this old memory and belief:

Age: ....

Memory: ....

....

....

....

....

....

How I felt: ....

What I needed: ....

....

....

....

....

Thought and new belief I can create to replace this old memory and belief:

....

....

....

....

....

....

Releasing Old Wounds and Narratives

Repeat after me: *I am not my chronic pain. I am not my chronic fatigue. I am not my wounds. I am not my trauma. I am not my symptoms. I am an immensely divine human who may be experiencing symptoms, but I am not them.*

For years, I've been speaking little self-fulfilling prophecies about myself, my body, and my life. Little lies that overtook my body, spreading like wildfire. I've also allowed others, especially practitioners and health specialists, to project their own self-fulfilling prophecies over me. I've carried the weight of all of this for my entire life.

My wounds, my trauma, and my conditions have defined me for my entire life. I've carried them with me as a means to define who I am, my identity. They've been somewhat of a security blanket because I wonder who I am without them. The ego has felt the need to keep them to allow me to feel safe.

So often, subconsciously, we attach to these things because we don't know who we are without them. I'm not saying you won't experience the ripple effects of your experiences within your body, nor will you be free of symptoms. It means you no longer need to carry the enormously heavy bag of projections. You can now put it down.

Repeat: *From this day forward, I make a conscious decision to put these down, and instead I step forward into my divine power and wisdom.*

Let's Continue to Disrupt and Dispel False Beliefs

How much of your time and energy is directed towards everything you can't do or towards limitations to do with your health, your wellbeing, your life, your financial status, your relationship status, and your friendships? A lot, I bet. For me, it would have been close to 90 percent.

Too much of our time is being invested in doing things and believing the 'can'ts', that is, the things that keep us trapped within this vicious cycle. So, I wrote down a list of things I wanted to stop investing my time in, and I realised that the list was exhaustive

I made a conscious decision to:
- Stop correlating success with being free of symptoms.
- Stop looking at symptoms as a failure.
- Stop looking for others to validate me.
- Stop chasing practitioners to justify symptoms or to fix me.
- Stop trying to find someone to blame.
- Stop focusing on my limitations.
- Stop psychoanalysing every single symptom.
- Stop hating on myself.
- Stop needing to fix myself at every point in my life.
- Stop blaming the world for the injustices and instead feel them and then release them.
- Stop putting limitations on myself.
- Stop with the victim mentality.
- Stop concerning myself with what other people think about me.
- Stop judging myself.

- Stop focusing on my body's inadequacies.
- Stop focusing on the cannots.

Instead, I started focusing on the positive 'cans':
- How I can approach each day.
- How I can eat foods that nourish my body.
- Gratitude.
- Quieting the mind.
- Learning how to support my nervous system.
- Getting to know who I am.
- Moving my body, even if it's just for five minutes.
- Breaking through mental blocks.
- Goal setting.
- Visualising my future in a positive manner.
- Creating joy and laughter in my life.
- Simplifying tasks.
- Fewer appointments.
- Doing more of what I love.
- Surrounding myself with positive people.

Take the time to write a list of the things you want to release and the things you would like to introduce and welcome into your life.

Note: take the time to feel the difference between when you say you can't, along with how this restricts us mentally, physically, and emotionally, and when we start to say we can, as well as how this starts to feel more expansive and liberating. This is the energy we want to start encompassing.

I also gave myself permission to:
- Just be me.
- Feel.
- Feel angry.
- Feel happiness and joy.
- Dream of new possibilities.
- Believe in new possibilities.

Now list all the areas where you give yourself permission to be uniquely you.

I give myself permission to…

Challenging Yourself out of Your Comfort Zone

We've touched on boundaries and saying no. That's right – we must learn how to say no. Many of us people-pleasing individuals have fallen into patterns where we don't know how to say no. We don't know how to say no to practitioners and specialists; we don't know how to say no to family members and friends, so we fall into vicious cycles of people-pleasing because, ultimately, we just want to be heard, to be validated, to be accepted, to be helped and guided. More often than not, these are the people who can't deliver this to you, and that's ok. It may not be in their capacity, or it may not be their job.

For some of us, we don't even know what we need, and when we don't know what we need, we can't expect others to fulfil or provide this.

Ask yourself these questions:

What boundaries do I need to set for myself? For example, stronger boundaries around personal space, better boundaries with practitioners and verbalising what I want or saying no to what I don't want, better boundaries with challenging myself out of my comfort zone.

What do I need to let go of to support my body? For example, limiting beliefs, guilt for not achieving, loss and grief for having to say goodbye to certain aspects of my life, negative thoughts that hinder my ability to move forward, practitioners who don't align with my values, friends and family who don't support me.

What do I need to do to support my body? For example, have better resources to support my mental, emotional, and physical health, have better boundaries with inflammatory foods or alcohol, have better sleep patterns.

....

....

....

....

....

....

....

....

....

....

....

Everything changed when I stopped waiting for someone to rescue me and I instead became my own hero.

Pillar Four – Creating a Relationship with Yourself

What is your purpose, and why do you need to know what it is?

With many people, they believe that their purpose is to work 38 hours a week and make money. That thinking has its place, as we do need to pay the bills and fund our lifestyle, but we need to delve deeper. Understanding your own personal purpose – that is, your why for living or why you believe you exist – can help you prevail over the pain and health conditions you're facing. The energy of discovering and understanding your why for life overflows into all areas.

My intent each day is to live my life in a way that serves my body to heal, living a life full of abundance. Abundance is different for everyone; for me, it means freedom in all areas of my life. It means being able to live congruent to my values. It means honouring my dreams and desires. It means being myself without the need to hide and conform to other people's expectations of who I need to be. It also means being able to express myself. Last but not least, it most definitely means encompassing a life of fun, love, joy, and excitement for the things I do, making decisions that will serve me and allow me to live a life of abundance and freedom. It also means I can get super concrete with the decisions I make for my body.

For example, I can ask: How is what I'm doing serving my body? Is this what I require for my body right now as it heals? Am I placing too much pressure or expectation over myself? Am I sitting in a state of self-pity, or am I empowered in my choices?

> It's time to take back your power.

To embody a state of ownership, you need to feel and start to believe that you have control over some aspects of your life. Ask yourself:

- What can I take ownership of today?
- What can I commit to for myself today?
- How can I start to prioritise my relationship with myself and my body?

Learning to Like and Love Ourselves

As a society, we're becoming more disconnected and disenfranchised with ourselves. We're bombarded by judgement through mass marketing, subliminal advertising, and social media, and we must question how this constant judgement has impacted our relationship with ourselves and our ability to heal. Has this external judgment influenced how and what we see and believe about ourselves? At the end of the day, we need to get down and dirty and be honest about what we think about ourselves.

Leading with judgment doesn't serve anyone. When we lead with love, it changes everything, not just in our relationships with others but in ourselves and our body. Healing autoimmune conditions, healing pain, healing fibromyalgia, healing trauma, healing dysregulated nervous systems, healing mental health, healing old wounds means accepting all the shadow parts of us that we've been taught to reject. It means knowing them and loving them as fundamentally part of us. There's no right or wrong because all those parts comprise the sum of who we are and how far we've come on this human journey.

Healing is learning to create loving bonds with each of these aspects of ourselves. Healing is developing relationships with all of these parts.

Take the time to look at your childhood and consider whether or not you've been taught to lead with love or with judgement. How has this influenced how you perceive and treat yourself and your body?

Write a list of all the parts of you that you've been taught to dislike, and make a commitment today to start accepting these parts of you.

I'll go first: parts of myself that I haven't liked about my body and have spoken negatively about for many years are small breasts, cellulite, far too strong legs, the wobbly parts around my stomach. Now it's your turn – write your own list of parts of yourself you've been taught to dislike and make a commitment to start accepting them today.

Reminding Ourselves of Our Unique Qualities

Sometimes, when too much of something has been in our reality, (for example, pain, negative thoughts, or emotions), it can take over, and we forget who we are without it. When we're diagnosed with a condition, it can often disrupt how we once saw ourselves and our existing identity, and we start to redefine ourselves with a new identity based around illness.

Just like the onion analogy, we need to strip back all of the layers, all of the masks and identities to remind ourselves of our key aspects. It's these things – the soul aspects – that create our uniqueness. They're also what we're generally good at and love.

We then need to identify how we can bring more of these aspects into our everyday lives and how we can find more of a cohesive balance where we start to become less defined by our disease, pain, and limitations. This is how you start to create your new reality and a new version of you (with the best of the old bits of you intertwined).

Circle the key attributes of who you are...

Sincere	Happy-go-lucky	Empathetic
Reliable	Careful	Brave
Easygoing	Creative	Warm
Friendly	Inquisitive	Calm
Perceptive	Technological	Sensitive
Communicative	Practical	Optimistic
Joyful	Problem solver	Curious
Cheerful	Diligent	Truthful
Sociable		

Change Your Story and Create Your Own Ending

Alongside all the different programs, narratives, and opinions you've received, you'll have created a story that adheres to them and limits you. For example, my narrative has been: "I will always be immunocompromised. I won't be able to work, nor exercise like I used to. I will always have fatigue. My symptoms will only worsen. I will be limited and have a life full of doctor and specialist appointments. I won't be able to work." This narrative ruled and dictated my life for so long.

I realised that I needed to break the spell, break the relationship I had with these programs and stories and make a conscious decision not to allow them to be spoken over me and to dictate my life and existence. Instead, I made a conscious choice to create a new narrative that served me so much better.

My new narrative consists of:
- Running around and playing with my kids.
- Being present within my everyday life.
- Being active and strong.
- Having a fulfilling career.
- Growing my own produce to nourish my body.
- Having community around me.
- Having nourishing, soulful relationships.
- Watching sunsets.
- Creating new experiences with travel.
- Being abundant in every single aspect of my life.
- Finding amazing practitioners who believe in my body's innate ability to heal.

- Having a strong, healthy body.
- Doing the things that I love.

Write your own new narrative, including your ideal ending. Then take steps to make it a reality. Remember, it's your story, so you have ultimate control.

INTEGRATED HEALING SUMMARISED

To summarise, as you begin your healing journey, it's important to remember the six rules you need to break:

- There is a one-size-fits-all approach to healing.
- Healing is linear.
- Life is only about healing.
- Life is a race.
- Letting go (detoxing) is easy.
- Compare yourself to the old days.

Once you know the rules, the ones that won't serve you on your healing journey, you can consciously break them. They'll become the foundation for everything that comes next.

Upon that foundation, we place the four pillars of disrupting pain:

- Understanding and releasing emotions
- Rebuilding your nervous system
- Reducing toxic load
- Creating a relationship with yourself

By **understanding and releasing emotions**, you reduce the emotional load and put yourself in a better space mentally to begin healing. Your mindset, your belief systems, your fears can all be reprogrammed to better serve you on your healing journey.

As we know, the experience of consistent and prolonged pain puts a lot of stress on the nervous system. To effectively heal, we must find ways to mitigate that stress through adequate rest, connection, and doing the things that make us feel good. It's about getting out of your own way, reducing what your body perceives to be stressful, and **rebuilding your nervous system**.

Additionally, **reducing toxic load** in the body is essential to the healing process. Unmet childhood needs, negative thoughts, unresolved trauma, genetics, modern life, and exposure to chemicals can all contribute to the burden on our body and our mind, and reducing that toxic load often requires a mindset shift and some lifestyle changes.

Finally, by **creating a relationship with yourself,** you can learn to like and love yourself and create a new narrative that serves you well in living the life you deserve, regardless of where you may be within your healing journey, knowing that you have always been enough. The power resides within you.

DON'T BE AFRAID TO BREAK THE RULES

> All of what you need is within you, and sometimes we just need a little guidance to bring us back to remembering who we fundamentally are.

That's what this book is: a journey to unlearning what you once knew, of breaking all the rules that you've associated with your pain, whether that be mental, physical, or emotional, of destroying whatever is limiting you or keeping you from moving forward and achieving the things you desire.

Pain is present for a myriad of reasons. Society has taught us to dismiss pain, to take a pill to suppress it, and to be at war with it. We're discovering that this doesn't work. Conventional treatment for long-term pain simply hasn't worked, so we need to look at how we can approach pain differently. Instead of simply trying to suppress the pain (like we have with so many other things), we need to start listening to our body's cues and ask why the pain is present. Simply suppressing any type of pain, whether physical, emotional, or mental, won't serve us because the cause hasn't been addressed.

Breaking the Rules of Pain asks for you to take back ownership and control. Asking why your pain is there and delving into its cause is pivotal. Are you sitting in a pattern of avoidance? Are you sitting within a victim mentality? Is your pain trying to tell you something? Is it trying to teach you something and guide you somewhere? How can you start to befriend your pain? How can you start to befriend your body?

For so long, we've associated pain with weakness – but this is a lie.

You are not weak.

You are strong, courageous, and empowered.

You are not broken.

You no longer need to be defined and dictated by your illness and your symptoms.

Your body is *for* you, not against you. She is your biggest ally and friend. She is your biggest advocate, and she wants the very best for you. Dismantle anything that says otherwise.

Although your mind can lead you astray and tell you lies due to feeling scared and unsafe, you're now aware of this, and you know why it occurs. Help yourself to reframe and reprogram any fear that may surface in your mind. Validate your fears, but don't allow them to take control of your mind and body. Remind yourself that you don't need to play these games and that you are safe.

Remember, your words have immense potency over what occurs in your body, so be mindful and kind to yourself.

You have the power – you always have. This means that you also have choice over what you do for yourself and your body. Make decisions that are aligned to what your body needs, rather than acting on fear.

Remain curious with yourself, your body, and be open to

different treatments and possibilities. Not one person will have the answer, and sometimes, as we heal, we may feel like we're going backwards when, in fact, we aren't. Give yourself a lot of grace and do the same for others when they get it wrong.

Put down your weapons. There's no need to be at war with yourself. Stop fighting yourself, your symptoms, and the world around you. Connect deeply within yourself and tell yourself you can surrender the need to be at continual war. From this day forward, make a commitment to bring forth harmony and peace into all your cells and into every aspect of your life.

Healing isn't linear, and there's no timeline, so you don't need to rush through it. The wonderful thing about this book is that the prompts are there for you to use in your own time and your own pace. Learn to feel into what this looks like for you.

Healing doesn't necessarily mean being free from disease or pain – so you can set aside that expectation now. Instead, learn to love and accept where you are on any given day. When you no longer feel that you need to control every aspect of your body and mind, it's liberating.

Healing and doing the work can be incredibly hard and can trigger and bring up even more emotions, but it can also be extremely rewarding knowing that you have the power and wisdom to restore balance to your body. Often, we can become so overburdened with the enormity of how much we need to do or the actions we need to take that our mind and nervous system becomes overwhelmed. Throughout this journey, if you become triggered and your heart and mind need extra support, be sure to reach out to those who can support you. This is not a sign of weakness but a sign of strength and courage. Be courageous!

Don't focus so much on the entire journey – just place one step in front of the other. That's all you need to do. Please be gentle with yourself and know that not every little thing needs to be healed immediately, nor is this realistic. Allow for time and space – and a lot of rest and stillness.

Allow for emotions to surface, knowing that there's no right, nor wrong. Watch them like an observer but with no judgement attached to what you're experiencing or how you've been taught to act or think or behave when you have emotions. Instead, just simply sit with them, start to connect with them. Open up your heart space and ask why they're there and if there's anything they need to tell you. You'll be surprised at what you discover.

Remember, you have all the wisdom and power within you, but, over the course of your life, you've lost trust in yourself and your body. This is simply the start of you returning back to yourself and discovering a deeper, more profound relationship with yourself.

Don't be afraid to break the rules of pain. I believe in you. You're stronger than you think. Enjoy the magic.

To connect with me and access additional resources and services, please visit amierule.com.au.

Acknowledgements

To acknowledge all those who have assisted me on my healing journey, to the practitioners, the wisdom keepers, the friends, the guides, my family who helped me to fulfil my dreams of writing this book, and ultimately to those who have guided me to return back to myself – the list is profound, and I can't simply thank you all within a few pages.

But as a starting point, to my beautiful children – Ethan and Zoe. You are my biggest teachers, and every day you remind me to humble myself, to open my eyes to new perspectives, to live carefree, and to love and laugh. May you always follow your heart. May you always realise that, despite the hardships you may face in life, you have choice, you are loved, and you only need to believe in yourselves.

To my husband Rhys, whom I fell in love with and married within a blink of an eye. You allowed me to open my heart like no other, to never be ashamed of who I am but to cherish it. You taught me what unconditional love truly is, to advocate for what I believe in, and to always follow my heart and dreams. I am honoured that I get to walk hand in hand with you as we create our life together.

To my mum and dad for giving me life and opportunity. Thank you for your endless love and support. To my mum especially – thank you for helping me break generational cycles and for all the hours and days and years you have sat with me and believed in me. You have known about my lifelong dream to write a book, and even though it has taken me decades, it's here. We planted the seed nearly three decades ago and have watered her slowly, yet surely.

To my lifelong friend Ellen Barker. You've known about my desires to write this book from day dot and have supported and cheered me on endlessly.

To Emma Carew-Reid – you are one of the most inspirational people I know.

To Cassidy Carey – my chronic pain endo friend and warrior. Thank you for walking the chronic pain journey alongside me, for sharing all aspects of your vulnerable self with me, and for being true to yourself. This book is for you too. I see how hard the walk of chronic pain is for you, and I commend you for all that you do for yourself.

To Emme Reeves – thank you for being you. I adore you beyond words and for teaching me to always be my weird and wonderful authentic self and for always giving me a hug when I need one.

To Polly Wagstaff – the most amazing kinesiologist. You have been there through some of the hardest times in my life, walking alongside me to heal generations of deep-seated trauma, to restore my body and learn to love myself once again. Thank you for your magic and friendship.

To Michelle Lithgow – although you have passed and are no longer in this world, you were one of my greatest inspirations. Autoimmune consumed a lot of your life, as did cancer. Yet you showed up every day regardless. We talked about health and treatment and the hardships of living with chronic conditions. I miss our long conversations, and I miss you more than you could imagine.

To Sherif Samir Riad – one of the most educated men yet so humble. You really taught me how the body holds the score, that is, how trauma and abuse is held so deeply within the subconscious aspects of ourselves and trapped within the body. Before I met you, I gave up hope and never thought I would be free of the stronghold that abuse can have. Never did I think this was possible, yet you guided me and taught me to trust in myself and the world. Thank you endlessly.

To Natalie Bird – thank you for your wisdom, your love and support, your friendship, your beautiful positive perspective on life, and your amazing hands that, for years, adjusted me and my kids with your chiropractic care. I learnt so much from you in how to restore my nervous system. Thank you for going beyond. I love you.

To Mark Pheely – one of the most beautiful souls I've ever met and the most profound yoga teacher. Through your lessons and teachings at Westside Yoga, you taught us the importance of connecting back to our inner wisdom. You were the catalyst for me to explore deeper on the path of learning, to trust who I was, and to rely on that wisdom. My heart is forever grateful for meeting and knowing you.

To Sophie Taua'i – creative director of Sophie Co, who so beautifully articulated my vision for all things branding and helped me to replicate this vision into my front cover. Thank you.

To the ever patient and amazingly experienced team at Dean Publishing. What a journey with many delays from my end due to personal and health issues. From the powerhouse Susan Dean, to the editor in chief Natalie Deane, to the most amazing editor Suzan Dalziel. Thank you for holding my vision close to my heart for so many years, for embracing my story, and for helping me to articulate in this amazing format for the rest of the world to see. I appreciate you all.

To my clients who have entrusted me. I thank you and I hope and desire for each and every one of you to walk on the path of self-discovery as you return back and connect to yourself.

To everyone who reached for this book. Thank you for making this a possibility and allowing me to fulfil a lifelong dream.

About the Author

Amie Rule is a health and chronic pain coach with an interest in psychotherapy and understanding the impact of trauma on the mind, body, and spirit. After nearly a decade of struggling with chronic pervasive pain, she identified a gap in the market regarding how pain is perceived and approached, writing *Breaking the Rules of Pain* to address the gaps and challenges people with chronic health and autoimmune conditions face.

Amie has a bachelor's degree in psychology, with a focus on loss and grief. When working with clients, she uses a person-centred trauma-informed approach.

Amie lives with her husband and two children on the Mornington Peninsula.

Endnotes

Part 1

1. Center on the Developing Child 2019, 'Epigenetics and Child Development: How Children's Experiences Affect Their Genes', *Harvard University*, viewed 13 November 2023, https://developingchild.harvard.edu/resources/what-is-epigenetics-and-how-does-it-relate-to-child-development/.

Part 2

1. Harlow, HF 1958, 'The Nature of Love', *American Psychology*, vol 13, no 12, pp 673–685, doi.org/10.1037/h0047884.

2. Woodhouse, SS, Scott, JR, Hepworth, AD, & Cassidy, J 2020, 'Secure Base Provision: A New Approach to Examining Links Between Maternal Caregiving and Infant Attachment', *Child Development*, vol 91, no 1, pp e249–e265, doi:10.1111/cdev.13224.

3. Pfeifer, JH & Berkman, ET 2018, 'The Development of Self and Identity in Adolescence: Neural Evidence and Implications for a Value-Based Choice Perspective on Motivated Behavior', *Child Development Perspectives*, vol 12, no 3, pp 158–164, viewed 13 November 2023, doi.org/10.1111/cdep.12279.

4. Center for Substance Abuse Treatment 2014, 'Chapter 3, Understanding the Impact of Trauma', in *Trauma-Informed Care in Behavioral Health*

Services, SAMHSA, Rockvillle, Maryland, viewed 13 November 2023, https://www.ncbi.nlm.nih.gov/books/NBK207191/.

5   Ramirez, J, Guarner, F, Fernandez, LB, Maruy, A, Sdepanian, VL, & Cohen, H 2020, 'Antibiotics as Major Disruptors of Gut Microbiota', *Frontiers in Cellular and Infection Microbiology*, vol 10, viewed 13 November 2023, doi.org/10.3389/fcimb.2020.572912.

Part 3

1   Nowak, C 2018, '15 Incredible Things the Human Body Does Every Minute', *The Healthy*, viewed 13 November 2023, https://www.thehealthy.com/bodies/human-body-every-minute/.

2   Daniel, A 2023, '37 Weird Facts about the Human Body That Will Blow Your Mind', *Best Life*, viewed 13 November 2023, https://bestlifeonline.com/crazy-body-facts/.

3   Opfer, C & Troutner, A 2022, 'Does Your Body Really Replace Itself Every Seven Years?', *HowStuffWorks*, viewed 13 November, https://science.howstuffworks.com/life/cellular-microscopic/does-body-really-replace-seven-years.htm.

4   de Costa, C 2009, 'Childbed Fever: A Major Cause of Maternal Mortality', *O&G Magazine*, viewed 13 November 2023, https://www.ogmagazine.org.au/11/1-11/childbed-fever-major-cause-maternal-mortality/.

5   The University of Sydney 2021, 'Invisible Disabilities: They Are More Common Than You Think', Sydney, viewed 5 November 2023, https://www.sydney.edu.au/study/student-life/student-news/2021/09/14/invisible-disabilities--they-are-more-common-than-you-think.html.

6   William, A 2021, *Medical Medium: Secrets Behind Chronic and Mystery Illness and How to Finally Heal*, Hay House, California, p 26.

7   Bland, J 2014, *The Disease Delusion*, Harper, New York.

8   Australian Institute of Health and Wellness 2020, 'Chronic Pain in Australia', *Australian Government*, Canberra, viewed 13 November 2023, https://www.aihw.gov.au/getmedia/10434b6f-2147-46ab-b654-a90f05592d35/aihw-phe-267.pdf.

9   Dobson, J 2021, 'Invisible Illness and Measurability', *AMA Journal of*

Ethics, vol 23, no 7, pp e512–513, viewed 7 November 2023, 10.1001/amajethics.2021.512.

10 Bland, J 2014, *The Disease Delusion*, Harper, New York, p 21.

11 Collier, R 2018, 'A Short History of Pain Management', *Canadian Medical Association Journal*, vol 190, no 1, pp e26–e27, viewed 13 November 2023, doi.org/10.1503/cmaj.109-5523.

12 Clarke, A 2021, 'Invisible Disabilities on the Rise', *Infinity Community Solutions*, viewed 7 November 2023, https://infinitycs.org.au/2021/02/23/invisible-disabilities-on-the-rise/.

13 Dobson, J 2021, 'Invisible Illness and Measurability', *AMA Journal of Ethics*, vol 23, no 7, pp e512–513, viewed 7 November 2023, doi.org/10.1001/amajethics.2021.512.

14 Hunter, J, Wardle, J, AM, KK, Molodysky, E, & Ewer, T 2016, 'The Case for Establishing an Australasian Integrative Medicine Practice-Based Research Network', *Australian Family Physician*, vol 45, no 12, viewed 13 November 2023, https://www.racgp.org.au/afp/2016/december/the-case-for-establishing-an-australasian-integrat.

15 Myss, C 2011, *Why People Don't Heal, And How They Can*, Random House Australia, Melbourne.

16 Myss, C 2011, *Why People Don't Heal, And How They Can*, Random House Australia, Melbourne, p 44.

17 Ee, C, Templeman, K, Forth, A, Kotsirilos, V, Singleton, G, Deed, G, Dubois, S, Pirotta, M, Harnett, J, Myers, S, & Hunter, J 2021, 'Integrative Medicine in General Practice in Australia: A Mixed-Methods Study Exploring Education Pathways and Training Needs,' *Global Advances in Health and Medicine*, viewed 13 November 2023, doi.org/10.1177/21649561211037594.

18 Gannotta, R, Malik, S, Chan, AY, Urgun, K, Hsu, F, & Vadera, S 2018, 'Integrative Medicine as a Vital Component of Patient Care', *Cureus*, vol 10, no 8, p e3098, viewed 13 November 2023, doi.org/10.7759/cureus.3098.

19 Allied Health Professionals Australia n.d., 'What Is Allied Health?', viewed 13 November 2023, https://ahpa.com.au/what-is-allied-health/.

20 Morell, SF & Cowan, TS 2013, *The Nourishing Traditions Book of Baby & Child Care*, Newtrends Publishing, Brandywine, Maryland.

21 Llor, C & Bjerrum, L 2014, 'Antimicrobial Resistance: Risk Associated with Antibiotic Overuse and Initiatives to Reduce the Problem', *Therapeutic Advances in Drug Safety*, vol 5, no 6, pp 229–241, viewed 13 November 2023, 10.1177/2042098614554919.

22 Bland, J 2014, *The Disease Delusion*, Harper, New York, p 2.

23 Maté, G 2004, *When the Body Says No: The Cost of Hidden Stress*, Vintage Canada, Toronto.

24 Maté, G 2004, *When the Body Says No: The Cost of Hidden Stress*, Vintage Canada, Toronto.

25 Santos-Longhurst, A 2023, 'Understanding and Managing Chronic Inflammation', *Healthline*, viewed 13 November 2023, https://www.healthline.com/health/chronic-inflammation.

26 Hartwig, D & Hartwig, M 2014, *It Starts with Food*, Victory Belt Publishing, Las Vegas.

27 Santos-Longhurst, A 2023, 'Understanding and Managing Chronic Inflammation', *Healthline*, viewed 13 November 2023, https://www.healthline.com/health/chronic-inflammation.

28 Bland, J 2014, *The Disease Delusion*, Harper, New York, p 2.

29 Cheung, MK, Leung, TF, Tam, WH, Leung, ASY, Chan, OM, Ng, RWY, Yau, JWK, Yuen, LY, Tong, SLY, Ho, WCS, Yeung, ACM, Chen, Z, & Chan, PKS 2023, 'Development of the Early-Life Gut Microbiome and Associations with Eczema in a Prospective Chinese Cohort', *mSystems*, doi.org/10.1128/msystems.00521-23.

30 Merriam-Webster n.d. 'The History of "Disease"', viewed 13 November 2023, https://www.merriam-webster.com/words-at-play/word-history-of-disease.

31 Maté, G 2004, *When the Body Says No: The Cost of Hidden Stress*, Vintage Canada, Toronto.

32 Maté, G 2004, When the Body Says No: The Cost of Hidden Stress, Vintage Canada, Toronto.

33 Maté, G 2004, *When the Body Says No: The Cost of Hidden Stress*, Vintage

Canada, Toronto.

34 Renard, GR 2004, *The Disappearance of the Universe: Straight Talk about Illusions, Past Lives, Religion, Sex, Politics, and the Miracles of Forgiveness*, Hay House, Carlsbad, California.

35 Robertson, S 2022, 'What Is Neurotoxicity?', *News-Medical*, viewed 13 November 2023, https://www.news-medical.net/health/What-is-Neurotoxicity.aspx.

36 Liu, J & Lewis, G 2014, 'Environmental Toxicity and Poor Cognitive Outcomes in Children and Adults', *Journal of Environmental Health*, vol 76, no 6, pp 130–138, viewed 13 November 2023, https://www.ncbi.nlm.nih.gov/pmc/articles/PMC4247328/.

37 Smirnova, L, Hogberg, HT, Leist, M, & Hartung, T 2014, 'Developmental Neurotoxicity - Challenges in the 21st Century and In Vitro Opportunities', *ALTEX*, vol 31, no 2, pp 129–156, viewed 13 November, https://doi.org/10.14573/altex.1403271.

38 Villoldo, A 2016, *One Spirit Medicine*, Hay House, Carlsbad, California, p 8.

39 Hari, J 2018, *Lost Connections: Uncovering the Real Causes of Depression – and Unexpected Solutions*, Bloomsbury, London.

40 Collier, R 2018, 'A Short History of Pain Management', Canadian Medical Association Journal, vol 190, no 1, pp e26–e27, viewed 13 November 2023, doi.org/10.1503/cmaj.109-5523.

41 World Health Organization 2022, 'Mental Health', viewed 13 November 2023, https://www.who.int/news-room/fact-sheets/detail/mental-health-strengthening-our-response.

42 Parliament of Australia n.d. 'Appendix 1 - Definitions of Mental Health and Mental Illness', viewed 13 November 2023,

https://www.aph.gov.au/Parliamentary_Business/Committees/Senate/Former_Committees/mentalhealth/report/e01.

43 Kenez, S, O'Halloran, P, & Liamputtong, P 2015, 'The Portrayal of Mental Health in Australian Daily Newspapers', *Australian and New Zealand Journal of Public Health*, vol 39, no 6, pp 513–517, viewed 13 November, doi.org/10.1111/1753-6405.12441.

44 Hari, J 2018, *Lost Connections: Uncovering the Real Causes of Depression – and the Unexpected Solutions*, Bloomsbury Publishing, London.

45 Halverson, JL 2023, 'Depression Clinical Presentation', Medscape, viewed 13 November 2023, https://www.medscape.com/answers/286759-14692/what-are-the-dsm-5-criteria-for-diagnosis-of-major-depressive-disorder-clinical-depression.

46 Maffei, ME 2020, 'Fibromyalgia: Recent Advances in Diagnosis, Classification, Pharmacotherapy and Alternative Remedies', *International Journal of Molecular Sciences*, vol 21, no 21, viewed 14 November 2023, https://doi.org/10.3390/ijms21217877.

47 Higuera, V 2023, '6 Possible Causes of Brain Fog', *Healthline*, viewed 14 November 2023, https://www.healthline.com/health/brain-fog.

48 Sankowski, R, Mader, S, & Valdés-Ferrer, SI 2015, 'Systemic Inflammation and the Brain: Novel Roles of Genetic, Molecular, and Environmental Cues as Drivers of Neurodegeneration', *Frontiers in Cellular Neuroscience*, vol 9, no 28, viewed 14 November 2023, https://doi.org/10.3389/fncel.2015.00028.

49 Hartwig, D & Hartwig, M 2014, *It Starts with Food*, Victory Belt Publishing, Las Vegas.

50 Sankowski, R, Mader, S, & Valdés-Ferrer, SI 2015, 'Systemic Inflammation and the Brain: Novel Roles of Genetic, Molecular, and Environmental Cues as Drivers of Neurodegeneration', *Frontiers in Cellular Neuroscience*, vol 9, no 28, viewed 14 November 2023, https://doi.org/10.3389/fncel.2015.00028.

51 Chen, D & Robinson, L 2020, 'Chronic Pain Patients "Suffering Unnecessarily" Call for Urgent Solution to National Specialist Shortage', *ABC News*, viewed 14 November 2023, https://www.abc.net.au/news/2020-11-10/national-pain-management-specialist-shortage-urgent-call/12840152.

52 PainAustralia 2021, 'Budget Submission 2021 to 2022: Working Together to Address Chronic Pain', viewed 19 September 2024, https://treasury.gov.au/sites/default/files/2021-05/171663_painaustralia_0.pdf.

53 Sontag, S 2014, *Illness as Metaphor and AIDS and Its Metaphors*, Penguin Random House, Melbourne.

54 McAllister, MJ n.d., 'How to End the Stigma of Pain', *Institute for Chronic Pain*, viewed 14 November 2023, https://www.instituteforchronicpain.org/understanding-chronic-pain/healthcare-system-failings/how-to-end-the-stigma-of-pain.

55 Virant, KW 2019, 'Chronic Illness and Shame', *Psychology Today*, viewed 19 September 2019, https://www.psychologytoday.com/au/blog/chronically-me/201903/chronic-illness-and-shame.

56 Curran, J 2007, 'Illness as Metaphor; AIDS and Its Metaphors', *British Medical Journal*, vol 335, no 7618, p 517, viewed 7 November 2023, doi.org/10.1136/bmj.39325.562176.94.

57 Abramson, A 2020, 'The Science of Shame', *Medium*, viewed 19 September 2024, https://elemental.medium.com/the-science-of-shame-e1cb32f6f2a.

Part 4

1 Corey, G 2001, *Theory and Practice of Counseling and Psychotherapy*, 6th edition, Brooks/Cole.

2 Maté, G 2004, *When the Body Says No: The Cost of Hidden Stress*, Vintage Canada, Toronto, p 37.

3 Maté, G 2004, *When the Body Says No: The Cost of Hidden Stress*, Vintage Canada, Toronto, p 37.

4 Sarno, JE 2001, *The Mind/Body Prescription: Healing the Body, Healing the Pain*, Grand Central Publishing, New York City, p 17.

5 Harris, R 2022, *The Happiness Trap: How to Stop Struggling and Start Living*, Shambhala, Boulder.

6 Brown, B 2013, 'Shame vs. Guilt', *BreneBrown.com*, viewed 20 September 2024, https://brenebrown.com/articles/2013/01/15/shame-v-guilt/.

7 Selva, J 2018, 'Why Shame and Guilt Are Functional for Mental Health', *PositivePsychology*, viewed 20 September 2024, https://positivepsychology.com/shame-guilt/.

8 Gordon, A 2021, *The Way Out: The Revolutionary, Scientifically Proven Approach to Heal Chronic Pain*, Vermilion, London, p 43.

www.ingramcontent.com/pod-product-compliance
Lightning Source LLC
Chambersburg PA
CBHW030253100526
44590CB00012B/383